The Poetry of John Greenleaf Whittier

A Readers' Edition

Edited and Introduced by
William Jolliff

Friends United Press
Richmond, Indiana
www.fum.org

Poems in this edition selected from *The Complete Poetical Works of John Greenleaf Whittier*. Ed. Horace E. Scudder. Boston and New York: Houghton Mifflin, 1894. (Cambridge Edition)

Book design by Julia Jensen.

Library of Congress Cataloging-in-Publication Data

Whittier, John Greenleaf, 1807-1892.
  [Poems. Selections]
  The poetry of John Greenleaf Whittier: a readers' edition / edited and with an introduction by William Jolliff.
      p. cm.
  Includes bibliographical references.
  ISBN 0-944350-48-8
      I. Jolliff, William. II. Title.

PS3252.J65 2000
811'.3--dc21   00-037585

This edition is dedicated to my children,
Jacob Henry, Rebecca Peace, and Anna Fulton,
and to my students at George Fox University,
with love and with hope.

I am grateful to George Fox University
for a faculty development grant which
allowed this work to be completed.
— William Jolliff

Contents

Foreword

William Jolliff has written the best short
introduction to Whittier as a man and
artist that readers have had in many
decades. His graceful and thoughtful essay on
Whittier's life, which opens this volume of poetic
selections, focuses on internal paradoxes that make
Whittier so interesting for the biographer and
historian.

Unlike Robert Penn Warren, an earlier editor
who presented a Whittier tortured by lost loves,
Jolliff sees Whittier as a man inhabited by a domi-
nant Quaker religious bent. This moral center
pulled him in one direction, while his creative
instincts and passionate ambition drove him after
poetic and political fame. Jolliff explores the ten-
sions that resulted from these conflicts and places
his interpretation solidly within historical and
biographical realities. He finds that Whittier's
dedication to abolitionism put him "in the refining
fire that his poetry needed" and that "by his sacrifi-
cial commitment [to the abolitionist cause] he

gained purpose, and that purpose could be integrated with the religious fabric of his psyche."

Jolliff has organized his selections in four thematic groupings: the crusading political prophet, the nostalgic recorder of a vanished rural past, the hardy balladeer of New England history, and the contemplative Quaker mystic. All the sections have sensitive introductions; a suggestive headnote introduces each poem. These headnotes offer persuasive comments on why Whittier's poems remain valuable for present-day readers.

Of "Mary Garvin" Jolliff remarks: "It seems at first glance to be a pleasant but unlikely interweaving of legend and soap opera....What sets this story apart is the theological tension in which Whittier situates the adventure....Some critics might argue that this is a romance spoiled by a theological conclusion, but such a claim ignores the very center of Whittier's being: that deeply religious core that came to inform all of his mature work."

Of the often ridiculed "In School Days" Jolliff remarks: "Read as a reflection of nineteenth-century gender rules or even old fashioned educational practices, this poem is a little unsettling. But if we forgive the poet his era...and hear what the poem says about innocence and love and self-sacrifice, something within it strikes at our core." Suggestive and thoughtful remarks like these characterize the headnotes and serve as a beguiling but still critical introduction to the poems themselves.

Finally, Jolliff writes with a gift for an apt and evocative phrase and the ability to get at the

essence of a poem or an idea succinctly. This
volume not only makes Whittier accessible to both
the general reader and the literary scholar, but also
offers sound critical, and often intriguing, reasons
why he should be read.

John B. Pickard
Editor, *The Whittier Newsletter*

Thine truly

John G. Whittier

An Introduction

John Greenleaf Whittier
The Man and the Poet

A day in the life of a
New England farm boy, circa 1820:

He rises before the sun, swallows a few mouthfuls of bread, and ambles off to the barn. As the dawn begins to glow, he is working alongside his father and brother, caring for the animals. He milks cows, feeds and waters livestock, and spreads fresh bedding in every stall and pen. That done, he stops back at the house for a more substantial breakfast, then hikes a mile to a one-room district school—if a teacher is available to hold the session.

When the closing bell rings, the boy's workday is far from over. The end of class means a long trek home and yet another stretch of labor in the fields or barns. Long after dark, he sits down with his family for a simple supper. After the leftovers are put away and the dishes cleared, the most treasured part of the day begins. He joins the family circle for an hour or two around the hearth, the very heart of the household. First they pray together, then they talk or read by the light of a tallow candle. If all is well, he'll doze off to tales of days gone by or equally splendid stories of days that never were.

If such a sentimental scene can be forgiven here, it is only because John Greenleaf Whittier himself bears no small responsibility for it. He was born in 1807 on just such a farm, he came of age in that "Era of Good Feelings" that followed the War of 1812, and his boyhood provided material for much of his best poetry. Captured in thousands of winsome, rhyming lines—most memorably his popular masterpiece, *Snow-Bound*—Whittier's images remain the most enduring portrait of domestic life during that idyllic time. Nearly two hundred years after his birth, his romantic vision remains the type that informs the stereotype. His boyhood persists as part of the American mind: whether you have read his poems or not, his picture is your picture.

And the picture is true, but it is not the whole truth. The farms of Essex County, Massachusetts, were poor, and it was only by strict economy and hard work that any living could be made.

The labor was so strenuous, in fact, that at seventeen Whittier was permanently injured with the strain of over-work, and he never fully recovered. No wonder he came to comfort himself with such early verses as "…must I always swing the flail, / And help to fill the milking pail? / I wish to go away to school; / I do not wish to be a fool." Still, half a century later, he would present the softened portrayal, and it remains a part of our cultural heritage.

ii

What kind of man emerges from such a childhood? Rufus Jones tells us that the mature Whittier was surrounded by "a peace beyond comprehension" and "a radiance of nature such as we attribute to the saint." Certainly such testimony bears weight; after all, Jones not only studied Whittier's work but met him and spoke with him. His witness certainly corresponds to the impression the portrait artists have given. It fits the image of the dark-eyed, snowy-bearded, mystical grandpa whose portrait once levitated above so many American school rooms. That he achieved the graceful contentment his painters and admirers have portrayed seems likely enough, but such an end came only as the last mile of a difficult journey.

Far from contented, a better adjective to describe Whittier for most of his life is *determined*, or, to put it less kindly, *driven*. He was driven first by his own ambition to discover a life beyond the Haverhill farm—a selfish goal by his own standards. And he was driven by a controlling need, encouraged by his Quaker heritage, to do good: to serve God by serving his fellow humans. Yet his inward struggle was more complex than that simple dialectic. To rightly consider the young poet's turmoil within, we need to keep in mind the fact that in his Quaker expression itself were two fundamental drives. His faith tradition had a moral passion that demanded action in the world; and his faith had a contemplative passion that invited an inward, mystical turning. Into this difficult mix, too, must be stirred the fact that he was a man of intense creative passion, and that he, like so many artists, wanted his work to reflect "eternal goodness."

But even this analysis is simplistic. In reality, these areas are not discrete; quite the contrary, they are all religious expressions. Quaker Christianity was the dominant informing and integrating force in his life, and beyond any particular struggle was the grander struggle to achieve and maintain the integration of the passions of his life and his faith. The fruit of the inward conflict, as well as the conflict itself, can be seen in the progression of his poetry. When his work began to mature in the 1850s, what characterized it was the thoroughness of his Christian vision, whether he was writing about abolition, his boyhood, the New England past, or his theology.

iii

The poet's earliest American ancestor, though not a Quaker, was certainly a man of deeply held religious opinions—and he paid a price for expressing them. In 1652, the courageous Thomas Whittier was stripped of his voting rights for dissenting publicly from the actions of his Puritan neighbors: he protested the persecution of Quakers. Within a generation, his family had married into the sect, and his descendants would become people of Friendly simplicity and devotion.

That was certainly true of Whittier's immediate household, which consisted of the poet's parents, John and Abigail, along with his siblings Mary, Matthew Franklin, and Elizabeth; his paternal uncle, Moses; and his maternal aunt, Mercy. They worshiped daily in the home, and twice each week the family made the nine-mile trek to the Amesbury meetinghouse, regardless of weather. Their bookshelf too, though a short one, reflected a Quaker heritage, featuring not only the Bible but standard works of Quaker writers such as Penn and Fox, Baxter and Chalkley, writers whose devotion to God and simplicity of style would be passed on to the Whittiers' literary son. Such a family created the poet's context for understanding what it meant to be Quaker, to be Christian, to live in such a way that faith becomes the very fabric of which life is sewn.

iv

Though the home was the dominant educating agent in his life, Whittier did attend district school during its brief yearly sessions. The quality of instruction was often poor, but it was not always so, and it was as a district school master that Joshua Coffin entered the Whittiers' circle. Like Whittier, Coffin would become an active abolitionist, and the student and the teacher became life-long friends. Just as importantly, it was through Coffin, and his generosity of a loaned book, that Whittier became acquainted with the poetry of Robert Burns. Though he had heard a few of Burns's verses recited by an itinerant Scot who had come to beg a meal, it was of Coffin's reading at the family fireside that Whittier would later say, "It was about the first poetry I ever heard . . . and it had a lasting influence on me." The rustic boy could hardly have found a more appropriate model for turning the stuff of everyday life into the stuff of poetry: like Whittier, Burns was a farmer, he lacked much formal education, and he voiced a keen awareness of social injustice. And Burns could not have fallen into the candlelight of a more energetic devotee: long before he had any idea what he was doing, Whittier was churning out poem after poem.

In those days, verse, often amateurish verse, was a standard feature of nearly every newspaper, a fact that proved fortunate for the ambitious Whittier. Unknown to the poet, his elder sister Mary appropriated one of his poems, "The Exile's Departure," signed it with a simple "W," and contributed it to the poetry column of the *Newburyport Free Press*. Not only did the editor print it, but he asked for more, a request Whittier, now aware of his sister's scheme, was only too happy to fulfill. So impressed was the paper's editor that, having discovered from the letter carrier the origin of the "W" poems, he drove to the Whittier farm. He wanted to meet the boy poet who, as he had claimed in a note that appeared with Whittier's second publication, "The Deity," "bears the stamp of true poetic genius."

As important as first publications are for a young writer, more significant is the fact that through these, two great leaders of the abolitionist movement would meet. For the supportive editor from Newburyport was William Lloyd Garrison, the activist who would become the foremost leader of radical abolitionism. Without his influence, the shape of Whittier's life—and the lives of thousands of others—would have been decisively changed. But great things often have inauspicious beginnings. At the moment of Garrison's unexpected arrival, the shy young poet was unpoetically crawling beneath the barn, collecting eggs from a hen which had moved her nest.

Garrison, always the reformer, had apparently come not only to meet the poet but to exhort his father concerning the importance of formal education. To his cheeky admonitions, the senior Whittier responded with Quaker simplicity: "Sir, poetry will not get him bread." Indeed, it would be forty years before poetry alone would supply the poet a living.

V

Nevertheless, Whittier was ambitious, and his father consented to allow him to raise money to attend a new school opening in Haverhill. By making women's slippers and selling them for eight cents a pair, he saved enough to begin his education off the farm. So at last when Haverhill Academy opened in 1827, at the head of the procession walked not one but two poets: Robert Dinsmore, a local celebrity whose imitations of Burns were widely known; and John Greenleaf Whittier, the new student who had been asked to write a dedicatory ode for the new institution. Through his years at the academy, Whittier, in addition to studying, working at odd jobs, and considerable socializing, was writing and publishing scores of poems in the newspapers, and a few

were even reprinted by more substantial periodi-
cals.

Though his time at the academy was brief, it was
important. He did his best to condense a high
school education into two terms, and just as impor-
tantly, he began to discover the ways of the world
off the farm. Due at least in part to his local literary
fame, he found social acceptance from leading
families in the town, made many friends, and fell
in love at least once. But at the same time, he
began to sense certain particularities about himself
which set him apart from his contemporaries, chief
among them his Quakerism. Though he immersed
himself in the world beyond his father's farm, he
took his faith with him, and it would remain a
constant and complicating force.

vi

Two terms at Haverhill Academy would prove to
be the extent of Whittier's formal education.
Money was unavailable for college, and he refused
to borrow or beg. The alternative was to find work,
and that he did. Again Garrison helped, this time
by supplying connections, and Whittier was soon
on his way to Boston to edit the *National Philan-
thropist.* Some changes with the publisher's plans,
however, resulted in Whittier arriving to find
himself editor of the *American Manufacturer,* a
political newspaper committed to supporting a
protective tariff, promoting American industry, and
forwarding the platform of Whig political positions.

Though he must have been disappointed,
Whittier made the adjustment skillfully. In his

newly assigned position, he learned all phases of
the newspaper business, from writing pointedly
partisan articles to setting his own type. Ultimately
the strain proved too much for his health—a
precarious variable throughout his life—and he
resigned the position after a few successful months.
This sequence became a pattern that would be
repeated throughout the first half of Whittier's life:
a short, often distinguished stint at editing such
papers as the *Essex Gazette*, the *New England Weekly
Review*, the *Pennsylvania Freeman*, and the *Middlesex
Standard*, a breakdown, then months of recuperat-
ing or working on the farm, or later, at his Ames-
bury home.

vii

Though today the two paths would hardly seem
complementary, while Whittier was building his
reputation as a fiery partisan political editor, he
was also seeking fame as a poet. In fact, he was
writing and publishing bushels of poetry, none of it
very good. The young Whittier had taken as his
original poetic hero Robert Burns, and he imitated
him for some time, as well as imitating Robert
Dinsmore, whose own work was patterned after
Burns's. But the Scottish elements of Burns's work
may ultimately have made him a less approachable
model than the other British romantics, especially
Scott and Byron. Less fortunately, Whittier also
continued to enjoy many of his American contem-
poraries, the newspaper poets of the day, most of
whom did nothing to improve the apprentice
poet's taste. Whittier was never sophisticated in his

literary judgment. He frankly admired the work of most poets who succeeded in gaining the fame he so ardently sought, many of whom wrote about a manner of life, and often with a shallowness of purpose, incompatible with Whittier's religious faith.

It seems likely then that although Whittier could—and did—achieve a certain local success by attempting to follow the path of the British romantics and their American imitators, he could never have maintained personal integrity or, for that matter, come to artistic maturity by following these models. He had neither the brilliance nor conscience of Scott and Byron, and he had far more artistic potential than the lesser artists. As a result, he suffered significant anxiety, though it is doubtful that he discovered its source; more consciously, he seems only to have realized that his poetry was not bringing him the kind of success he thought at times he wanted: fame, financial security, possibly even marriage to some sophisticated young woman. He was aware of his own ambition, so much so that he once wrote to a friend that he wished to be known in a "loftier capacity than as a writer of rhymes" and to another that he was "haunted by an immediate ambition," driven by "a very foolish desire of distinction, of applause, of fame, of what the world calls immortality."

viii

Partisan newspaper editing at first may have been little more than a way to hold his body and soul together and to help support his family while he pursued the phantom of literary fame. As a journalist, though, he became familiar with the pleasures of politics, enjoyed the inebriation of influence, and, as time went on, even gained a command of the subtle intricacies of political maneuvering. So when distinction as a poet and journalist seemed too long in coming and too unlikely to supply the material situation he wanted, Whittier set his sights on a political career. His newspaper work had schooled him for such a pursuit: he knew the issues of this day, and he circulated within a range of acquaintances that must have seemed broad indeed to the farmer's son. But it is just as important that political involvement by its very nature demanded that he champion some cause or causes, and thus prescribed a kind of moral pose that may have seemed easier to interweave with his Quakerism than was the writing of verses—a profession which tended to focus on the self, and, in Whittier's case, not the best self.

In time, his political experience would serve him well as a lobbyist for abolition; but before being put to that noble use, it led through experiences during which the struggling Quaker lost sight of the Inward Light. Or, at the very least, the magnetism of errant ambition interfered with his moral compass. One clear example occurred in 1832. Whittier, convinced that such a position would give him the successful start he needed, wanted very badly to be elected to the Massachusetts legislature. He knew that he had considerable support, but he also knew that he was a few weeks under age. To circumvent the restriction, Whittier connived and conspired to delay the finalizing of the election beyond his birthday. Worse yet, he did so by promising the spoils of office to his political friends. Without apparent embarrassment, he solicited Edwin Harriman and assured him that "I never yet deserted a friend, and I never will. If my friends enable me to acquire influence, it shall be exerted for their benefit." Clearly he planned to use the ugly practice of distributing political favors—a practice he had often condemned as an editor.

The implications of such actions better reflect politics as usual than the Quaker tenet of plain speech. Not only was he compromised, but, as if to salt the wound with righteousness, he failed to gain the office. This incident suggests how close Whittier might have come to leading a very different life than the one for which he is esteemed today. Yet we may imagine that even when he maintained the idealistic angle of the crusading political worker, his careerism, his personal ambition, still made Whittier uneasy. Such anxiety with the man he was becoming may have made him more ready, some months later, to turn his life toward a worthier goal.

ix

With the advantage of hindsight, it seems obvious that selfish ambition, whether political or literary, would prove a short-lived motivator for Whittier, as indeed it did. Striving for political prestige could not be integrated with Whittier's heartfelt Quaker principles. Something had to change, and the change seems to have been brought about in the spring of 1833, when William Lloyd Garrison once again entered Whittier's life. Having determined to champion the cause of abolition, Garrison sent Whittier a note that included this typical flourish: "Whittier enlist!—Your talents, zeal, influence—all are needed."

Such an emphatic call was just what was needed by the energetic but badly focused young man. By turning his energies toward abolition, Whittier could pursue, as energetically as his personality demanded, a goal not only worthwhile in his own conscience, but worthy of his Quaker heritage as well, a heritage that actively advocated the equality of all people. It was the opportunity to drive himself toward excellence and even some notoriety, while at the same time offering his life as a sacrifice for the good of humanity.

His formal conversion to the cause was confirmed that year by his attendance at the American Anti-Slavery Society convention, where Whittier signed his name to the gathering's declaration of principles. As the poet would reflect decades later, "I am not insensible to literary reputation. I love, perhaps too well, the praise and good-will of my fellow-men; but I set a higher value on my name as appended to the Anti-Slavery Declaration of 1833 than on the title-page of any book." Soon after, he wrote the pamphlet *Justice and Expediency*. That tract was more than a useful synopsis of arguments against slavery. Widely reprinted and circulated, it was the publication that would brand

Whittier as a radical for decades to come. It would limit his range of professional possibilities, it would close a good many social doors, and it would place him in real physical danger on more than one occasion from violent mobs. But it would also commit him to a life's work that was, by its very nature, in harmony with the most essential elements of his religious world view.

The significance of the change was not lost on Whittier, though we may assume that the fullest understanding of his dedication to abolition came only with time. Some years later he wrote to the British abolitionist Joseph Sturge, "This cause [abolition] has been to me what the vision on the house-top of Cornelius was to Peter—it has destroyed all narrow sectarian prejudices, and made me willing to be a man among men." So much was he a "man among men" that a casual overview of his life after he responded to the "calling" of abolition might not seem to reveal much change. He still took part in political lobbying, wrote voluminously, and occasionally took up editing responsibilities as well. But in addition he traveled throughout New England, attending conventions and shaping their purposes; he tirelessly circulated and presented petitions; and he generally sought out and performed any task he could imagine to further the cause of abolition. Whatever his formal occupation, his vocation was focused toward a single purpose. When he edited, it was for the abolitionist cause; when he lobbied, it was on behalf of the slave; even when he applied rather un-Quakerly pressure to certain politicians, it was for that single holy purpose. And, most importantly, when he wrote, whether poetry or prose, his work was not the faded copy of a distant, romantic model; he composed with the courage and authenticity of a man whose every energy is integrated in the service of his ultimate concern.

In material terms, Whittier was no more, probably considerably less, successful than he would have been had he chosen a more moderate path. But all his driving energy, not simply his career, had gained direction with his commitment to the cause of the slave. And that ability to align passion, compassion, and religious conviction would soon carry over into his poetry, regardless the topic. As a result, the self-conscious meanderings of his apprentice work soon fell away, replaced by the straightforward footsteps of commitment.

X

Late in life, Whittier wrote to E.L. Godkin that he was "grateful to the Divine Providence that so early called my attention to the great interest of humanity, saving me from the poor ambitions and miserable jealousies of a selfish pursuit of literary reputation." As noted above, the truth is that by the time he found his true vocation, he had already exercised himself in pursuing his "poor ambitions" and had not been as successful as he would have liked. He had worked diligently, even selfishly, not only as a poet but as a journalist and politician, and his work had not been, by his own estimates, sufficiently compensated. Thus when, as he later reflected, he "left the Muses' haunts to turn / The crank of an opinion-mill, / Making his rustic reed of song / A weapon in the war with wrong," his choice was not driven by religious devotion alone but by a general anxiety with the direction of his life. This does not diminish the quality of his sacrifice from a personal perspective: Whittier chose not to follow his passion for poetry or his equal passion for literary fame. But in assessing his renunciation for the sake of abolition, one cannot help but recall the words of Jesus: "He that loseth his life for my sake shall find it."

Most assuredly, Whittier found it. From the perspective of literary history, when Whittier gave up literary ambitions to give his life to the cause of liberty, he was not depriving the world of a major contribution. His early published work was not very good, and, appraised from a distance, showed but little promise. He was an efficient versifier who could turn out lines quickly on some variety of topics or occasions, but little more. There is nothing lasting—or even particularly edifying—in his early work. One can understand why the poet who wrote *Snow-Bound* might indeed wish, in his old age, to destroy the work of the poet who wrote "The Exile's Departure"—even if that poet is an earlier version of himself. Those early poems not only lacked focus, they lacked the kind of vital content and engagement that would allow focus to develop. His conversion to abolition, then, was crucial: in exchanging the life of personal ambition for the life of a reformer, Whittier was putting himself in the refining fire that his poetry needed. By his sacrificial commitment, he gained purpose, and that purpose was one that could be integrated with the religious fabric of his psyche.

That Whittier's weakest work was the work of his vital youth seems to go against the grain of the popular understanding of romantic poets. In considering a Wordsworth, a Keats, or a Byron, we celebrate their early brilliance. But Whittier was never brilliant, early or late. His lasting worth abides in his deep and thoughtful religious devotion, and while poetic brilliance comes early, a mature religious integration of life and work does not. One might even suggest, rather seriously, that Whittier became a great poet at least in part because he managed, in spite of poor health, to live and work a very long time.

It was not until the late 1840s and 1850s that the first excellent poems were written. Although abolition was still very much an issue and a topic for Whittier's poetry during this time, by the 1850s his most active period of political involvement had passed. A more settled life allowed his focus more frequently to include literary excellence. As a result, this was not only the period in which he wrote his best abolitionist poetry; it was also the period in which he began to write his best historical and sentimental poetry and his first great religious poetry. As a contributing editor to the *National Era*, he had a ready market for his work, and, just as important, he had the freedom to stay in Amesbury—which he did. In the decade of association with that paper, he published between its covers some one hundred poems and three hundred pieces of prose. Still more notably, the *Era* published some of his very first mature work, pieces such as "Ichabod," "Official Piety," "The

Haschish," "Mabel Martin," "Trust," and "Trinitas."
Still broader circulation came with the creation of a
new journal, when in 1857 Whittier's book pub-
lisher James T. Fields, along with a handful of the
most distinguished literary men of Boston, started
the *Atlantic Monthly*. From its first number, it was a
prestigious literary outlet, and one that allowed
Whittier a wider and more cultivated audience
than he had ever experienced, an audience that
could appreciate—and expect—such poems as
"Telling the Bees," "My Playmate," "The Old
Burying Ground,""Skipper Ireson's Ride," and "My
Psalm."

Though Whittier came into his artistic maturity
in the 1850s, it would be still another decade
before he would gain the popular success he had
once longed for. But when it came, it came in a
flood.

In August of 1865 he wrote to Fields that he was
writing "a homely picture of old New England
times. If I ever finish I hope and trust it will be
tolerably good." The work referred to is *Snow-
Bound*, and good it was. Not only was it Whittier's
acknowledged masterpiece, but by a rare and
happy concurrence, it was a popular and financial
triumph as well. Published in 1866, the poem
found a ready audience in a nation torn by civil
war and seeking healing. Whittier's "winter idyll"
was just the relief the ailing public needed from
the presentiment that life would never be quite so
good again as it was, or may have been, when the
family was gathered in the cabin on the farm,
waiting out the storm in the warmth of the hearth
fire. Within a month and a half of its publication,

ten thousand copies were sold, and by the year's end, the number had reached twenty-five thousand. The first edition netted Whittier ten thousand dollars—quite a fortune for a man who had seldom made more than a few hundred dollars per year.

Though now in his sixties, Whittier was enjoying a productive period as a poet, along with his first great financial success. For the first time he could live comfortably on the income from his poetry, and he did his best to redeem the time. In the twenty-five years between the success of *Snow-Bound* and his death in 1892, he published another half-dozen original collections of poems, edited several more volumes, and saw the Riverside Edition of his *Collected Works* through publication. Though such a full success had been a long time in coming, the farmer boy—who had struggled with his own ambition to make a place for himself beyond the Haverhill homestead—had succeeded: his name was a household word. The partisan editor who felt called to do God's will by turning his every energy to the abolitionist cause had seen his efforts come to fruition: slavery was done. And most importantly, the driven Christian who had felt persistently that calling to artistic excellence, but suppressed it for the sake of a cause, suddenly found himself the master of a powerful artistic instrument. His romantic passion had been disciplined, his craft refined: at last the Quaker mystic had the time, the financial security, and the mastery to transform the fruit of his inward journey into art.

Little wonder, then, that a devotional depth began more explicitly to characterize his work in the maturity of his career. It is safe to say that his faith had been informing his art from the time he turned his energy toward the most worthy cause he could discover. His dedication to justice allowed him to experience an integrity of art and faith, regardless of the topic considered. But as secular concerns at last began to fall away, his works became clearly spiritual not only in intention but in subject matter as well. The best religious poems of his final decades came as compensation for a long and strenuous inward journey.

xi

Although interest in Whittier, like interest in the other "schoolroom poets," has waned in the twentieth century, many contemporaries are nevertheless attracted to Whittier the poet through their admiration for Whittier the activist. Still others are drawn by the handful of masterworks still anthologized in textbooks: *Snow-Bound,* "Ichabod," "Telling the Bees," and a few others. Unfortunately the reader who, thus introduced, borrows the collected poetry from the library will not likely get beyond the first twenty pages. Two things immediately become apparent: Whittier wrote a daunting amount of poetry, and most of it is not very good. Such an evaluation would have been no news to Whittier. Although he was not a man of great literary taste, and though he was given to praise the work of others too strongly, he was aware of the weaknesses of his work. In fact, he omitted hundreds of poems from his authorized editions, and most likely would have sifted more had he not believed—and accurately—that someone, out of greed or devotion, would have published them anyway, in one form or another.

That said, he also wrote an abundance of excellent poetry—probably as much readable poetry as any nineteenth century American other than Emily Dickinson and Walt Whitman. And these poems should be read. My purpose, then, in this edition, has been to choose poems on the basis of a single criterion: their intrinsic excellence. My measure has been the pleasure they would give literate contemporary readers—my students, my colleagues, my neighbors. The happy fact is that once the distractions of the bad verse are removed, a weighty volume remains of work that reads very well indeed by any standard, whether of Whittier's century or our own.

Proem

**[Written to introduce the first general
collection of Whittier's Poems]**

I LOVE the old melodious lays
Which softly melt the ages through,
  The songs of Spenser's golden days,
  Arcadian Sidney's silvery phrase,
Sprinkling our noon of time with freshest
    morning dew.

  Yet, vainly in my quiet hours
To breathe their marvellous notes I try;
  I feel them, as the leaves and flowers
  In silence feel the dewy showers,
And drink with glad, still lips the blessing of
    the sky.

  The rigor of a frozen clime,
The harshness of an untaught ear,
  The jarring words of one whose rhyme
  Beat often Labor's hurried time,
Or Duty's rugged march through storm and
    strife, are here.

25

Of mystic beauty, dreamy grace,
No rounded art the lack supplies;
  Unskilled the subtle lines to trace,
  Or softer shades of Nature's face,
I view her common forms with unanointed
     eyes.

  Nor mine the seer-like power to show
The secrets of the heart and mind;
  To drop the plummet-line below
  Our common world of joy and woe,
A more intense despair or brighter hope to
     find.

  Yet here at least an earnest sense
Of human right and weal is shown;
  A hate of tyranny intense,
  And hearty in its vehemence,
As if my brother's pain and sorrow were my
     own.

  O Freedom! if to me belong
Nor mighty Milton's gift divine,
  Nor Marvell's wit and graceful song,
  Still with a love as deep and strong
As theirs, I lay, like them, my best gifts on thy
     shrine!

          Amesbury, 11th mo., 1847.

I.
Prophet to the Republic

"The Christian Slave" and Other Tirades

In all but a few instances, this edition includes two sets of introductory notes for each poem. William Jolliff's notes appear before the title of each poem. John Greenleaf Whittier's original notes appear in smaller type, indented, below the title of the poem.
–*Ed.*

J ohn Greenleaf Whittier made a commitment and paid the price. When he presented his life to the war against slavery, he offered the abolitionist banner all the persuasive and artistic talent at his disposal—and all at a moment's notice. When necessity joined with passion to lessen his artistic power, when his rhetorical choices drew him toward doggerel and away from literary excellence, he considered the exchange well made. Not his own literary reputation but the hearts and minds of his readers—how they felt and how he wanted them to feel—were the primary focus of his work. His calling was to awaken conscience and inspire action.

More surprising than the occasional mediocrity of some of his verse is its frequent excellence. From the standpoint of literary distinction, Whittier's abolitionist pledge should have set a doomed course. After all, political writing seldom outlives the cause it was written to serve. A few scholars of popular culture may still recall temperance jingles, suffragist polemics, and campaign choruses, but such are seldom featured in collections of great literature. So it is a rare achievement that so many of Whittier's poems insist on holding their place among literary masterworks. Apparently the habit of craft—along with the occasional visitation of genius—overcame the predictable weaknesses of poems that were seldom intended to be more than newspaper verse. And certainly the infectious energy of a full-throated, single-minded determination never loses its appeal—it lends these poems a power that crosses the centuries.

No writer has ever been more committed to a cause than was Whittier to the end of slavery. And though he despised the institution part and parcel, his hottest anger was always centered on that peculiar American harmonizing of slavery and Christianity. Given these convictions, it is no surprise that he voiced nothing short of contempt for clergy who failed to oppose that evil practice— and they were legion, not only in the South but in the poet's native New England as well. As a Quaker, Whittier put little stock in clerics or priests—a special class of "men of God"—in the first place, but for such professionally holy ones to earn their "hire" with "the price of blood" was more than he could stand. To his credit, Whittier usually managed to hate the sin and love the sinner. But, like the prophets of the Old Testament, he ladled out his most vicious invective on anyone who by action or apathy oppressed the poor—in this case, the poor slaves.

Clerical Oppressors

In the report of the celebrated pro-slavery meeting in Charleston, S.C., on the 4th of the ninth month, 1835, published in *Courier* of that city, it is stated: "The clergy of all denominations attended in a body, lending their sanction to the proceedings, and adding by their presence to the impressive character of the scene!"

JUST God! and these are they
Who minister at thine altar, God of Right!
Men who their hands with prayer and
blessing lay
On Israel's Ark of light!

What! preach, and kidnap men?
Give thanks, and rob thy own afflicted poor?
Talk of thy glorious liberty, and then
Bolt hard the captive's door?

What! servants of thy own
Merciful Son, who came to seek and save
The homeless and the outcast, fettering down
The tasked and plundered slave!

Pilate and Herod, friends!
Chief priests and rulers, as of old, combine!
Just God and holy! is that church, which
lends
Strength to the spoiler, thine?

Paid hypocrites, who turn
Judgment aside, and rob the Holy Book

Of those high words of truth which search
     and burn
  In warning and rebuke;

  Feed fat, ye locusts, feed!
And, in your tasselled pulpits, thank the Lord
That, from the toiling bondman's utter need,
  Ye pile your own full board.

  How long, 0 Lord! how long
Shall such a priesthood barter truth away,
And in Thy name, for robbery and wrong
  At Thy own altars pray?

  Is not Thy hand stretched forth
Visibly in the heavens, to awe and smite?
Shall not the living God of all the earth,
  And heaven above, do right?

  Woe, then, to all who grind
Their brethren of a common Father down!
To all who plunder from the immortal mind
  Its bright and glorious crown!

  Woe to the priesthood! woe
To those whose hire is with the price of blood;
Perverting, darkening, changing, as they go,
  The searching truths of God!

  Their glory and their might
Shall perish; and their very names shall be
Vile before all the people, in the light
  Of a world's liberty.

Oh, speed the moment on
When Wrong shall cease, and Liberty and
Love
And Truth and Right throughout the earth be
known
As in their home above.

Whittier's poems reveal that he found it easier even to excuse slave-owners for their misguided practice than to forgive those elements of the church that would lend religious support to such barbarism. "The Christian Slave" is powerfully imbued with his righteous indignation. That a child of God would be sold—and for a higher price—because she is a Christian—that was the most bitter of ironies. Little wonder his sarcasm turns to prayer, and finally to the question, "How long, O God, how long?"

The Christian Slave

In a publication of L. F. Tasistro – *Random Shots and Southern Breezes* – is a description of a slave auction at New Orleans, at which the auctioneer recommended the woman on the stand as "A Good Christian!" It was not uncommon to see advertisements of slaves for sale, in which they were described as pious or as members of the church. In one advertisement a slave was noted as "a Baptist Preacher."

A CHRISTIAN! going, gone!
Who bids for God's own image? for his grace,
Which that poor victim of the market-place,
    Hath in her suffering won?

    My God! can such things be?
Hast Thou not said that whatsoe'er is done
Unto Thy weakest and Thy humblest one
    Is even done to Thee?

    In that sad victim, then,
Child of Thy pitying love, I see Thee stand;
Once more the jest-word of a mocking band,
    Bound, sold, and scourged again!

    A Christian up for sale!
Wet with her blood your whips, o'ertask her
        frame,
Make her life loathsome with your wrong and
        shame,
    Her patience shall not fail!

    A heathen hand might deal
Back on your heads the gathered wrong of
        years:
But her low, broken prayer and nightly tears,
    Ye neither heed nor feel.

    Con well thy lesson o'er,
Thou prudent teacher, tell the toiling slave
No dangerous tale of Him who came to save
    The outcast and the poor.

But wisely shut the ray
Of God's free Gospel from her simple heart,
And to her darkened mind alone impart
    One stern command, Obey!

So shalt thou deftly raise
The market price of human flesh; and while
On thee, their pampered guest, the planters
        smile,
    Thy church shall praise.

Grave, reverend men shall tell
From Northern pulpits how thy work was blest,
While in that vile South Sodom first and best,
    Thy poor disciples sell.

Oh shame! the Moslem thrall,
Who, with his master, to the Prophet kneels,
While turning to the sacred Kebla feels
    His fetters break and fall.

Cheers for the turbaned Bey
Of robber-peopled Tunis! he hath torn
The dark slave-dungeons open, and hath
        borne
    Their inmates into day:

But our poor slave in vain
Turns to the Christian shrine his aching eyes;
Its rites will only swell his market price,
    And rivet on his chain.

God of all right! how long
Shall priestly robbers at Thine altar stand,
Lifting in prayer to Thee the bloody hand
    And haughty brow of wrong?

Oh, from the fields of cane,
From the low rice-swamp, from the trader's
            cell;
From the black slave-ship's foul and
            loathsome hell,
    And coffle's weary chain;

Hoarse, horrible, and strong,
Rises to Heaven that agonizing cry,
Filling the arches of the hollow sky,
    How long, O God, how long?

                                        1843

Whittier's introduction to "Massachusetts to
    Virginia" tells the story of George Latimer,
the escaped slave whose capture brought about
this poem. The poet does not mention, however,
that the petitions of the Massachusetts citizens to
challenge Congress had little effect, and that soon
simultaneous conventions were held throughout
the state in protest. The Essex County meeting
held in Ipswich was treated to the first reading of
one of Whittier's greatest and most widely
circulated poems.

Massachusetts to Virginia

Written on reading an account of the proceedings of the citizens of Norfolk, Va., in reference to George Latimer, the alleged fugitive slave, who was seized in Boston without warrant at the request of James B. Grey, of Norfolk, claiming to be his master. The case caused great excitement North and South, and led to the presentation of a petition to Congress, signed by more than fifty thousand citizens of Massachusetts, calling for such laws and proposed amendments to the Constitution as should relieve the Commonwealth from all further participation in the crime of oppression. George Latimer himself was finally given free papers for the sum of four hundred dollars.

THE blast from Freedom's Northern hills, upon
   its Southern way,
Bears greeting to Virginia from Massachusetts
   Bay:
No word of haughty challenging, nor battle
   bugle's peal,
Nor steady tread of marching files, nor clang
   of horsemen's steel.

No trains of deep-mouthed cannon along
   our highways go;
Around our silent arsenals untrodden lies the
   snow;
And to the land-breeze of our ports, upon
   their errands far,
A thousand sails of commerce swell, but none
   are spread for war.

We hear thy threats, Virginia! thy stormy
      words and high
Swell harshly on the Southern winds which
      melt along our sky;
Yet, not one brown, hard hand foregoes its
      honest labor here,
No hewer of our mountain oaks suspends his
      axe in fear.

Wild are the waves which lash the reefs along
      St. George's bank;
Cold on the shores of Labrador the fog lies
      white and dank;
Through storm, and wave, and blinding mist,
      stout are the hearts which man
The fishing-smacks of Marblehead, the sea
      boats of Cape Ann.

The cold north light and wintry sun glare on
      their icy forms,
Bent grimly o'er their straining lines or
      wrestling with the storms;
Free as the winds they drive before, rough as
      the waves they roam,
They laugh to scorn the slaver's threat against
      their rocky home.

What means the Old Dominion? Hath she
      forgot the day
When o'er her conquered valleys swept the
      Briton's steel array?
How side by side, with sons of hers, the
      Massachusetts men

Encountered Tarleton's charge of fire, and
      stout Cornwallis, then?

Forgets she how the Bay State, in answer to
      the call
Of her old House of Burgesses, spoke out from
      Faneuil Hall ?
When, echoing back her Henry's cry, came
      pulsing on each breath
Of Northern winds the thrilling sounds of
      "Liberty or Death!"

What asks the Old Dominion? If now her sons
      have proved
False to their fathers' memory, false to the
      faith they loved;
If she can scoff at Freedom, and its great
      charter spurn,
Must we of Massachusetts from truth and
      duty turn?

We hunt your bondmen, flying from Slavery's
      hateful hell;
Our voices, at your bidding, take up the
      bloodhound's yell;
We gather, at your summons, above our
      fathers' graves,
From Freedom's holy altar-horns to tear your
      wretched slaves!

Thank God! not yet so vilely can
      Massachusetts bow;
The spirit of her early time is with her even
      now;

Dream not because her Pilgrim blood moves
slow and calm and cool,
She thus can stoop her chainless neck, a
sister's slave and tool!

All that a sister State should do, all that a free
State may,
Heart, hand, and purse we proffer, as in our
early day;
But that one dark loathsome burden ye must
stagger with alone,
And reap the bitter harvest which ye
yourselves have sown!

Hold, while ye may, your struggling slaves,
and burden God's free air
With woman's shriek beneath the lash, and
manhood's wild despair;
Cling closer to the "cleaving curse" that writes
upon your plains
The blasting of Almighty wrath against a land
of chains.

Still shame your gallant ancestry, the cavaliers
of old,
By watching round the shambles where
human flesh is sold;
Gloat o'er the new-born child, and count his
market value, when
The maddened mother's cry of woe shall
pierce the slaver's den!

Lower than plummet soundeth, sink the
Virginia name;

Plant, if ye will, your fathers' graves with
      rankest weeds of shame;
Be, if ye will, the scandal of God's fair
      universe;
We wash our hands forever of your sin and
      shame and curse.

A voice from lips whereon the coal from
      Freedom's shrine hath been,
Thrilled, as but yesterday, the hearts of
      Berkshire's mountain men:
The echoes of that solemn voice are sadly
      lingering still
In all our sunny valleys, on every windswept
      hill.

And when the prowling man-thief came
      hunting for his prey
Beneath the very shadow of Bunker's shaft of
      gray,
How, through the free lips of the son, the
      father's warning spoke;
How, from its bonds of trade and sect, the
      Pilgrim city broke!

A hundred thousand right arms were lifted
      up on high,
A hundred thousand voices sent back their
      loud reply;
Through the thronged towns of Essex the
      startling summons rang,
And up from bench and loom and wheel her
      young mechanics sprang!

41

The voice of free, broad Middlesex, of
> thousands as of one,
The shaft of Bunker calling to that of
> Lexington;
From Norfolk's ancient villages, from
> Plymouth's rocky bound
To where Nantucket feels the arms of ocean
> close her round;

From rich and rural Worcester, where through
> the calm repose
Of cultured vales and fringing woods the
> gentle Nashua flows,
To where Wachuset's wintry blasts the
> mountain larches stir,
Swelled up to Heaven the thrilling cry of "God
> save Latimer!"

And sandy Barnstable rose up, wet with the
> salt sea spray;
And Bristol sent her answering shout down
> Narragansett Bay!
Along the broad Connecticut old Hampden
> felt the thrill,
And the cheer of Hampshire's woodmen
> swept down from Holyoke Hill.

The voice of Massachusetts! Of her free sons
> and daughters,
Deep calling unto deep aloud, the sound of
> many waters!

Against the burden of that voice what tyrant
    power shall stand?
No fetters in the Bay State! No slave upon her
    land!

Look to it well, Virginians! In calmness we
    have borne,
In answer to our faith and trust, your insult
    and your scorn;
You've spurned our kindest counsels; you've
    hunted for our lives;
And shaken round our hearths and homes
    your manacles and gyves!

We wage no war, we lift no arm, we fling no
    torch within
The fire-damps of the quaking mine beneath
    your soil of sin;
We leave ye with your bondmen, to wrestle,
    while ye can,
With the strong upward tendencies and
    godlike soul of man!

But for us and for our children, the vow
    which we have given
For freedom and humanity is registered in
    heaven;
No slave-hunt in our borders,—no pirate on
    our strand!
No fetters in the Bay State,—no slave upon
    our land!

1843

Inspired by an article in the *National Era* about slave caravans, Whittier added yet another tonal color to his protest palette. In "Song of the Slaves in the Desert," the poet is neither frothing prophet nor lampooning social critic. In a mood of plaintive empathy, he crafts the sounds to characterize the lonely plight of the displaced slaves crying for their homeland. Such subtlety, especially in his expert manipulation of the refrain, is rare for Whittier. He creates a timbre that is both rich and plaintive, resulting in lines that cry to be sung. Keep in mind that although several African-American folk songs use the woman's name "Rubee," in this poem it is the word for "God" in the Mandara or Bornou language.

Song of Slaves in the Desert

WHERE are we going? where are we going,
    Where are we going, Rubee?
Lord of peoples, lord of lands,
Look across these shining sands,
Through the furnace of the noon,
Through the white light of the moon.
Strong the Ghiblee wind is blowing,
Strange and large the world is growing!
Speak and tell us where we are going,
    Where are we going, Rubee?

Bornou land was rich and good,
Wells of water, fields of food,
Dourra fields, and bloom of bean,
And the palm-tree cool and green:
Bornou land we see no longer,
Here we thirst and here we hunger,
Here the Moor-man smites in anger:
      Where are we going, Rubee?

When we went from Bornou land,
We were like the leaves and sand,
We were many, we are few;
Life has one, and death has two:
Whitened bones our path are showing,
Thou All-seeing, thou All-knowing!
Hear us, tell us, where are we going,
      Where are we going, Rubee?

Moons of marches from our eyes
Bornou land behind us lies;
Stranger round us day by day
Bends the desert circle gray;
Wild the waves of sand are flowing,
Hot the winds above them blowing,—
Lord of all things! where are we going?
      Where are we going, Rubee?

We are weak, but Thou art strong;
Short our lives, but Thine is long;
We are blind, but Thou hast eyes;
We are fools, but Thou art wise!
Thou, our morrow's pathway knowing
Through the strange world round us growing,

Hear us, tell us where are we going,
Where are we going, Rubee?

1847

Whittier's abolition poems are best known for their clear and infectious emotional animation. Such verses are meant to be shouted. But in "Ichabod," the poet takes a different stance. Faced with the circumstances described in the preface, Whittier swelled with righteous indignation. He felt betrayed. But instead of responding with poetic fire, he wrote a poem that voices pity for Webster, comparing him with that Old Testament character whose name means "Where is the glory?" Such a portrayal must have been more humiliating for Webster than the most profane attack. The tone of restraint and pity makes it one of Whittier's best, and most bitter, anti-slavery poems.

Ichabod

This poem was the outcome of the surprise and grief and forecast of evil consequences which I felt on reading the seventh of March speech of Daniel Webster in support of the "compromise," and the Fugitive Slave Law. No partisan or personal enmity dictated it. On the contrary my admiration of the splendid personality and intellectual power of the great Senator was never stronger than when I laid down his speech, and, in one of the saddest

moments of my life, penned my protest. I saw, as I
wrote, with painful clearness its sure results,—the
Slave Power arrogant and defiant, strengthened
and encouraged to carry out its scheme for the
extension of its baleful system, or the dissolution
of the Union, the guaranties of personal liberty in
the free States broken down, and the whole
country made the hunting-ground of slave-
catchers. In the horror of such a vision, so soon
fearfully fulfilled, if one spoke at all, he could only
speak in tones of stern and sorrowful rebuke.

But death softens all resentments, and the
consciousness of a common inheritance of frailty
and weakness modifies the severity of judgment.
Years after, in "The Lost Occasion," I gave utter-
ance to an almost universal regret that the great
statesman did not live to see the flag which he
loved trampled under the feet of Slavery, and, in
view of this desecration, make his last days glori-
ous in defense of "Liberty and Union, one and
inseparable."

So fallen! so lost! the light withdrawn
    Which once he wore!
The glory from his gray hairs gone
    Forevermore!

Revile him not, the Tempter hath
    A snare for all;
And pitying tears, not scorn and wrath,
    Befit his fall!

Oh, dumb be passion's stormy rage,
    When he who might
Have lighted up and led his age,
    Falls back in night.

Scorn! would the angels laugh, to mark
    A bright soul driven,
Fiend-goaded, down the endless dark,
    From hope and heaven!

Let not the land once proud of him
    Insult him now,
Nor brand with deeper shame his dim,
    Dishonored brow.

But let its humbled sons, instead,
    From sea to lake,
A long lament, as for the dead,
    In sadness make.

Of all we loved and honored, naught
    Save power remains;
A fallen angel's pride of thought,
    Still strong in chains.

All else is gone; from those great eyes
    The soul has fled:
When faith is lost, when honor dies,
    The man is dead!

Then, pay the reverence of old days
    To his dead fame;
Walk backward, with averted gaze,
    And hide the shame!

1850

It was clear to Whittier that any sensitive understanding of "higher" or "divine" law would demand the abolition of slavery. In fact as a Quaker, Whittier believed himself to be guided by a higher law, the Inward Light, in his work for abolition. So the very idea that the buying and selling of human beings was actually supported by a divine principle—by the will of God—was repulsive. Such perverse "piety," he believed, proved that "[s]in in high places has become devout." Even Satan, he suggests, surely "gives to God the praise" for such "monstrous progeny."

Official Piety

Suggested by reading a state paper, wherein the higher law is invoked to sustain the lower one.

A PIOUS magistrate! sound his praise
throughout
The wondering churches. Who shall
henceforth doubt
That the long-wished millennium draweth
nigh?
Sin in high places has become devout,
Tithes mint, goes painful-faced, and prays
its lie
Straight up to Heaven, and calls it piety!

The pirate, watching from his bloody deck
  The weltering galleon, heavy with the gold
Of Acapulco, holding death in check
  While prayers are said, brows crossed,
      and beads are told;
The robber, kneeling where the wayside cross
On dark Abruzzo tells of life's dread loss
From his own carbine, glancing still abroad
For some new victim, offering thanks to God!
  Rome, listening at her altars to the cry
Of midnight Murder, while her hounds of hell
Scour France, from baptized cannon and holy
      bell
  And thousand-throated priesthood, loud
      and high,
  Pealing Te Deums to the shuddering sky,
  "Thanks to the Lord, who giveth victory!"
What prove these, but that crime was ne'er so
      black
As ghostly cheer and pious thanks to lack?
Satan is modest. At Heaven's door he lays
His evil offspring, and, in Scriptural phrase
And saintly posture, gives to God the praise
And honor of the monstrous progeny.
What marvel, then, in our own time to see
His old devices, smoothly acted o'er,—
Official piety, locking fast the door
Of Hope against three million souls of men,—
Brothers, God's children, Christ's redeemed,—
      and then,
With uprolled eyeballs and on bended knee,
Whining a prayer for help to hide the key!
                 1853

That flawed understanding of divine law,
Whittier believed, resulted from a distorted
view of the gospel, a view so twisted that no one of
sober mind could accept it. But, as he comically
suggests in this poem, possibly Americans who
support slavery are intoxicated. Their vice, he
suggests, is not haschish (the flowering tops of the
hemp plant) but the intoxicating effects of another
plant—a plant that seems to make his countrymen
drunk with greed.

The Haschish

OF all that Orient lands can vaunt
    Of marvels with our own competing,
The strangest is the Haschish plant,
    And what will follow on its eating.

What pictures to the taster rise,
    Of Dervish or of Almeh dances!
Of Eblis, or of Paradise,
    Set all aglow with Houri glances!

The poppy visions of Cathay,
    The heavy beer-trance of the Suabian;
The wizard lights and demon play
    Of nights Walpurgis and Arabian!

The Mollah and the Christian dog
    Change place in mad metempsychosis;

The Muezzin climbs the synagogue,
  The Rabbi shakes his beard at Moses!

The Arab by his desert well
  Sits choosing from some Caliph's daughters,
And hears his single camel's bell
  Sound welcome to his regal quarters.

The Koran's reader makes complaint
  Of Shitan dancing on and off it;
The robber offers alms, the saint
  Drinks Tokay and blasphemes the Prophet.

Such scenes that Eastern plant awakes;
  But we have one ordained to beat it,
The Haschish of the West, which makes
  Or fools or knaves of all who eat it.

The preacher eats, and straight appears
  His Bible in a new translation;
Its angels negro overseers,
  And Heaven itself a snug plantation!

The man of peace, about whose dreams
  The sweet millennial angels cluster,
Tastes the mad weed, and plots and schemes,
  A raving Cuban filibuster!

The noisiest Democrat, with ease,
  It turns to Slavery's parish beadle;
The shrewdest statesman eats and sees
  Due southward point the polar needle.

The Judge partakes, and sits erelong
    Upon his bench a railing blackguard;
Decides off-hand that right is wrong,
    And reads the ten commandments
        backward.

O potent plant! so rare a taste
    Has never Turk or Gentoo gotten;
The hempen Haschish of the East
    Is powerless to our Western Cotton!

1854

Much of the political maneuvering that preceded the Civil War concerned the slave status of new western territory. Would new states be slave or free? And who would decide?

In "Letter From A Missionary," Whittier, always highly ecumenical when lambasting corruption in the church, speaks this time in the voice of a Methodist missionary who is furthering the gospel—the gospel of slavery, that is—to Kansas. Particularly gruesome is the fact that this missionary's "converts" help him chase down and kill runaway slaves. Any reader who sleeps through the sarcasm early in the poem should awaken with Whittier's venomous report that some of the converts "[h]ave purchased negroes, and are settling down / As sober Christians! Bless the Lord for this!" or revive with the final bit of wordplay (based on Matthew 7:3), "So *mote* it be."

Letter

FROM A MISSIONARY OF THE METHODIST EPISCOPAL
CHURCH SOUTH, IN KANSAS, TO A DISTINGUISHED POLITICIAN

Douglas Mission August, 1854.

Last week—the Lord be praised for all His mercies
To His unworthy servant !—I arrived
Safe at the Mission, via Westport where
I tarried over night, to aid in forming
A Vigilance Committee, to send back,
In shirts of tar, and feather-doublets quilted
With forty stripes save one, all Yankee comers,
Uncircumcised and Gentile, aliens from
The Commonwealth of Israel, who despise
The prize of the high calling of the saints,
Who plant amidst this heathen wilderness
Pure gospel institutions, sanctified
By patriarchal use. The meeting opened
With prayer, as was most fitting. Half an hour
Or thereaway, I groaned, and strove, and wrestled,
As Jacob did at Penuel, till the power
Fell on the people, and they cried "Amen!"
"Glory to God!" and stamped and clapped their
                    hands;
And the rough river boatmen wiped their eyes;
"Go it, old hoss!" they cried,and cursed the
                    niggers—
Fulfilling thus the word of prophecy,
"Cursëd be Canaan." After prayer, the meeting
Chose a committee—good and pious men—
A Presbyterian Elder, Baptist deacon,
A local preacher, three or four class-leaders,
Anxious inquirers, and renewed backsliders,

54

A score in all—to watch the river ferry,
(As they of old did watch the fords of Jordan,)
And cut off all whose Yankee tongues refuse
The Shibboleth of the Nebraska bill.
And then, in answer to repeated calls,
I gave a brief account of what I saw
In Washington; and truly many hearts
Rejoiced to know the President, and you
And all the Cabinet regularly hear
The gospel message of a Sunday morning,
Drinking with thirsty souls of the sincere
Milk of the Word. Glory! Amen, and Selah!

Here, at the Mission, all things have gone well:
The brother who, throughout my absence, acted
As overseer, assures me that the crops
Never were better. I have lost one negro,
A first-rate hand, but obstinate and sullen.
He ran away some time last spring, and hid
In the river timber. There my Indian converts
Found him, and treed and shot him. For the rest,
The heathens round about begin to feel
The influence of our pious ministrations
And works of love; and some of them already
Have purchased negroes, and are settling down
As sober Christians! Bless the Lord for this!
I know it will rejoice you. You, I hear,
Are on the eve of visiting Chicago,
To fight with the wild beasts of Ephesus,
Long John, and Dutch Free-Soilers. May your arm
Be clothed with strength, and on your tongue be
                    found
The sweet oil of persuasion. So desires
Your brother and co-laborer. Amen!

P. S. All's lost. Even while I write these lines
The Yankee abolitionists are coming
Upon us like a flood—grim, stalwart men,
Each face set like a flint of Plymouth Rock
Against our institutions—staking out
Their farm lots on the wooded Wakarusa,
Or squatting by the mellow-bottomed Kansas;
The pioneers of mightier multitudes,
The small rain-patter, ere the thunder shower
Drowns the dry prairies. Hope from man is not.
Oh, for a quiet berth at Washington,
Snug naval chaplaincy, or clerkship, where
These rumors of free labor and free soil
Might never meet me more. Better to be
Door-keeper in the White House, than to dwell
Amidst these Yankee tents, that, whitening, show
On the green prairie like a fleet becalmed.
Methinks I hear a voice come up the river
From those far bayous where the alligators
Mount guard around the camping filibusters:
"Shake off the dust of Kansas. Turn to Cuba—
(That golden orange just about to fall,
O'er-ripe, into the Democratic lap;)
Keep pace with Providence, or, as we say,
Manifest destiny. Go forth and follow
The message of *our* gospel, thither borne
Upon the point of Quitman's bowie knife,
And the persuasive lips of Colt's revolvers.
There may'st thou, underneath thy vine and fig-tree,
Watch thy increase of sugar cane and negroes,
Calm as a patriarch in his eastern tent!"
Amen: So mote it be. So prays your friend.

1854

56

In May of 1854, four days after the passage of the Kansas-Nebraska Bill fanned the flames of discontent concerning the spread of slavery, a meeting of the Boston Vigilance Committee was held. The topic of the day was the plight of Anthony Burns, a local clothing store employee who had been claimed as a runaway slave by his Virginia owner. The meeting came to an end when several white citizens, including Whittier's friends Wendell Phillips, Theodore Parker, and Thomas Wentworth Higginson, rushed to the courthouse to commandeer the slave's release. Authorities responded to the men's valiant if misguided effort with clubs and arrests. Though consistently opposed to violence, Whittier nevertheless wrote these lines in honor of his fellow abolitionists' "holy rage."

For Righteousness' Sake

Inscribed to friends under arrest for treason against the slave power.

THE age is dull and mean. Men creep,
    Not walk; with blood too pale and tame
    To pay the debt they owe to shame;
Buy cheap, sell dear; eat, drink, and sleep
    Down-pillowed, deaf to moaning want;
Pay tithes for soul-insurance; keep
    Six days to Mammon, one to Cant.

In such a time, give thanks to God,
    That somewhat of the holy rage
    With which the prophets in their age
On all its decent seemings trod,
    Has set your feet upon the lie,
That man and ox and soul and clod
    Are market stock to sell and buy!

The hot words from your lips, my own,
    To caution trained, might not repeat;
    But if some tares among the wheat
Of generous thought and deed were sown,
    No common wrong provoked your zeal;
The silken gauntlet that is thrown
    In such a quarrel rings like steel.

The brave old strife the fathers saw
    For Freedom calls for men again
    Like those who battled not in vain
For England's Charter, Alfred's law;
    And right of speech and trial just
Wage in your name their ancient war
    With venal courts and perjured trust.

God's ways seem dark, but, soon or late,
    They touch the shining hills of day;
    The evil cannot brook delay,
The good can well afford to wait.
    Give ermined knaves their hour of crime;
Ye have the future grand and great,
    The safe appeal of Truth to Time!

                                        1855

Just a year later, Massachusetts passed its "Personal Liberty Law," a piece of legislation which attempted to free the Bay State's citizenry from forced participation in the return of runaways. Whittier responded to the law with the following tribute.

Arisen At Last

On the passage of the bill to protect the rights and liberties of the people of the State against the Fugitive Slave Act.

I SAID I stood upon thy grave,
    My Mother State, when last the moon
    Of blossoms clomb the skies of June.

And, scattering ashes on my head,
    I wore, undreaming of relief,
    The sackcloth of thy shame and grief.

Again that moon of blossoms shines
    On leaf and flower and folded wing,
    And thou hast risen with the spring!

Once more thy strong maternal arms
    Are round about thy children flung,—
    A lioness that guards her young!

No threat is on thy closëd lips,
But in thine eye a power to smite
The mad wolf backward from its light.

Southward the baffled robber's track
Henceforth runs only; hereaway,
The fell lycanthrope finds no prey.

Henceforth, within thy sacred gates,
His first low howl shall downward draw
The thunder of thy righteous law.

Not mindless of thy trade and gain,
But, acting on the wiser plan,
Thou 'rt grown conservative of man.

So shalt thou clothe with life the hope,
Dream-painted on the sightless eyes
Of him who sang of Paradise,—

The vision of a Christian man,
In virtue, as in stature great
Embodied in a Christian State.

And thou, amidst thy sisterhood
Forbearing long, yet standing fast,
Shalt win their grateful thanks at last;

When North and South shall strive no more,
And all their feuds and fears be lost
In Freedom's holy Pentecost.

1855

It is safe to say that when it came to the truth in his narrative poetry, Whittier seems to have valued history more as material to be used for a high purpose than as data to be laboriously researched and chronicled. His main concern was for truth with a capital T. A poem like "Barbara Frietchie," thankfully, does not depend upon painstaking accuracy to be successful. Its accomplishment lies in Whittier's concrete, straightforward diction, his memorable meter, his vivid images, and his understanding of his audience. He knew that his readers wanted to see the Union—and the flag that represented it—honored and loved, not only by a fearless Yankee woman, but by a noble Confederate general.

Barbara Frietchie

This poem was written in strict conformity to the account of the incident as I had it from respectable and trustworthy sources. It has since been the subject of a good deal of conflicting testimony, and the story was probably incorrect in some of its details. It is admitted by all that Barbara Frietchie was no myth, but a worthy and highly esteemed gentlewoman, intensely loyal and a hater of the Slavery Rebellion, holding her Union flag sacred and keeping it with her Bible; that when the Confederates halted before her house, and entered her dooryard, she denounced them in vigorous language, shook her cane in their faces, and drove them out; and when General Burnside's troops

followed close upon Jackson's, she waved her flag
and cheered them. It is stated that May Quantrell,
a brave and loyal lady in another part of the city,
did wave her flag in sight of the Confederates. It is
possible that there has been a blending of the two
incidents.

Up from the meadows rich with corn,
Clear in the cool September morn,

The clustered spires of Frederick stand
Green-walled by the hills of Maryland.

Round about them orchards sweep,
Apple and peach tree fruited deep,

Fair as the garden of the Lord
To the eyes of the famished rebel horde,

On that pleasant morn of the early fall
When Lee marched over the mountain wall;

Over the mountains winding down,
Horse and foot, into Frederick town.

Forty flags with their silver stars,
Forty flags with their crimson bars,

Flapped in the morning wind: the sun
Of noon looked down, and saw not one.

Up rose old Barbara Frietchie then,
Bowed with her fourscore years and ten;

Bravest of all in Frederick town,
She took up the flag the men hauled down;

In her attic window the staff she set,
To show that one heart was loyal yet.

Up the street came the rebel tread,
Stonewall Jackson riding ahead.

Under his slouched hat left and right
He glanced; the old flag met his sight.

"Halt!"—the dust-brown ranks stood fast.
"Fire!"—out blazed the rifle-blast.

It shivered the window, pane and sash;
It rent the banner with seam and gash.

Quick, as it fell, from the broken staff
Dame Barbara snatched the silken scarf.

She leaned far out on the window-sill,
And shook it forth with a royal will.

"Shoot, if you must, this old gray head,
But spare your country's flag," she said.

A shade of sadness, a blush of shame,
Over the face of the leader came;

The nobler nature within him stirred
To life at that woman's deed and word;

"Who touches a hair of yon gray head
Dies like a dog! March on!" he said.

All day long through Frederick street
Sounded the tread of marching feet:

All day long that free flag tost
Over the heads of the rebel host.

Ever its torn folds rose and fell
On the loyal winds that loved it well;

And through the hill-gaps sunset light
Shone over it with a warm good-night.

Barbara Frietchie's work is o'er,
And the Rebel rides on his raids no more.

Honor to her! and let a tear
Fall, for her sake, on Stonewall's bier.

Over Barbara Frietchie's grave,
Flag of Freedom and Union, wave!

Peace and order and beauty draw
Round thy symbol of light and law;

And ever the stars above look down
On thy stars below in Frederick town!

1863

II.
The Warming Haze
of Yesterday

"Telling the Bees"
and Other Memories

As Whittier's audience grew, his fame came to rest increasingly on his accomplished images of a quickly disappearing rural life. He could step easily into the past and return with just what Americans needed. Lost in his verses, his readers would soon be living days "rich in flowers and trees, / Humming-birds and honey-bees." They would hear the "bleat of sheep along the hill" or a "bucket plashing in the cool sweet well." A "clover-smell in the breeze" would replace the city soot that darkened their changing air. A thousand shades of pastoral life were mixed on Whittier's palette, and no one used them with a richer result. Memory's images were all the more pleasing in light of the changes that his generation was witnessing. In the poet's boyhood, the great majority of Americans lived by farming; by 1860, nearly half the population in the northern states was urban. In 1820, 350,000 Americans worked in factories; by 1860, 2,000,000 Americans were factory or mill workers. Realistically, the family home no longer held the kind of dominant economic or social role it once had owned, and the results of the transformation were not only known in the mind but felt in the heart. Couple these changes with the national catastrophe of the Civil War, and it is little wonder that many Americans felt that somehow they had been cut adrift.

So they sought harbor in an earlier time. Even if, as the old saw goes, "nostalgia is the longing for a past which never existed," the poet understood the longings, if not all the reasons, of his thousands of devoted readers. Truth to tell, his own boyhood gave the lie to simple nostalgia. Those days were full of rigorous labor, and he had sought any honorable escape from work on the Essex County farm. That said, no one could recollect more vividly or with greater passion a "boyhood's pain-less play" or "sleep that wakes in laughing day." Hardships tend to melt away in the warmth of memory, and so it was with Whittier.

Even a cool century later, though, the appeal of his best poems still wakens something dozing inside us. When the details of his pastoral life are spun with the craft of the myth-maker, the result-ing pictures from the poet's past somehow feel like our own. Our "School-Days" may lack the roman-tic haze of Whittier's, but we can recall a moment here or an hour there with some of his fondness. And most of us did not experience the carefree childhood of the "Barefoot Boy," but then, neither did Whittier. Still, that child lived in him and lives in us. Possibly the persevering popularity of his work suggests a truth that supports his apparently old-fashioned sentimentality: simple goodness receives an open-armed reception in any genera-tion.

The way time rewrites perceptions is true not only of Whittier's memories of his boyhood, but of his understanding of relationships. Though he never married, throughout his life Whittier had many close, occasionally romantic, relationships with women. Yet even when his affections were reciprocated, he always seemed to find some reason not to marry—ill health, family responsibilities, professional pursuits, and sometimes even religious differences. In "Memories," he confesses that differing expressions of Christianity have come between his lover and himself: "wider yet in thought and deed / Diverge our pathways," he claims. We should not too easily, however, attribute the cooling of love to the differences between his lover's Calvinism ("the Genevan's sternest creed") and his own Quaker faith ("The Derby dalesman's simple truth"). Students of his life seem to agree that Whittier, though not quite a happy bachelor, rather enjoyed his unattached condition. Still, the strong emotions that challenged it often carried him to poetry.

Memories

A BEAUTIFUL and happy girl,
   With step as light as summer air,
Eyes glad with smiles, and brow of pearl,
Shadowed by many a careless curl
   Of unconfined and flowing hair;

A seeming child in everything,
    Save thoughtful brow and ripening charms,
As Nature wears the smile of Spring
    When sinking into Summer's arms.

A mind rejoicing in the light
    Which melted through its graceful bower,
Leaf after leaf, dew-moist and bright,
And stainless in its holy white,
    Unfolding like a morning flower:
A heart, which, like a fine-toned lute,
    With every breath of feeling woke,
And, even when the tongue was mute,
    From eye and lip in music spoke.

How thrills once more the lengthening chain
    Of memory, at the thought of thee!
Old hopes which long in dust have lain,
Old dreams, come thronging back again,
    And boyhood lives again in me;
I feel its glow upon my cheek,
    Its fulness of the heart is mine,
As when I leaned to hear thee speak,
    Or raised my doubtful eye to thine.

I hear again thy low replies,
    I feel thy arm within my own,
And timidly again uprise
The fringëd lids of hazel eyes,
    With soft brown tresses overblown.
Ah! memories of sweet summer eves,
    Of moonlit wave and willowy way,
Of stars and flowers, and dewy leaves,
    And smiles and tones more dear than they!

Ere this, thy quiet eye hath smiled
   My picture of thy youth to see,
When, half a woman, half a child,
Thy very artlessness beguiled,
   And folly's self seemed wise in thee;
I too can smile, when o'er that hour
   The lights of memory backward stream,
Yet feel the while that manhood's power
   Is vainer than my boyhood's dream.

Years have passed on, and left their trace,
   Of graver care and deeper thought;
And unto me the calm, cold face
Of manhood, and to thee the grace
   Of woman's pensive beauty brought.
More wide, perchance, for blame than praise,
   The school-boy's humble name has flown;
Thine, in the green and quiet ways
   Of unobtrusive goodness known.

And wider yet in thought and deed
   Diverge our pathways, one in youth;
Thine the Genevan's sternest creed,
While answers to my spirit's need
   The Derby dalesman's simple truth.
For thee, the priestly rite and prayer,
   And holy day, and solemn psalm;
For me, the silent reverence where
   My brethren gather, slow and calm.

Yet hath thy spirit left on me
   An impress Time has worn not out,
And something of myself in thee

71

A shadow from the past, I see,
    Lingering, even yet, thy way about;
Not wholly can the heart unlearn
    That lesson of its better hours,
Not yet has Time's dull footstep worn
    To common dust that path of flowers.

Thus, while at times before our eyes
    The shadows melt and fall apart,
And, smiling through them, round us lies
The warm light of our morning skies,—
    The Indian Summer of the heart!
In secret sympathies of mind,
    In founts of feeling which retain
Their pure, fresh flow, we yet may find
    Our early dreams not wholly vain!

                                        1843

Plagued throughout his life by poor health that limited his professional and personal ambitions, Whittier escaped the most uncomfortable weeks of summer by seeking the cool consolation of mountain air. And what comforted the body comforted the spirit as well. On the trip portrayed in "The Lakeside," Whittier discovers the "tender love" of God in "radiant hill and woodland dim, / And tinted sunset sea."

The Lakeside

THE shadows round the inland sea
    Are deepening into night;
Slow up the slopes of Ossipee
    They chase the lessening light.
Tired of the long day's blinding heat,
    I rest my languid eye,
Lake of the Hills! where, cool and sweet,
    Thy sunset waters lie!

Along the sky, in wavy lines,
    O'er isle and reach and bay,
Green-belted with eternal pines,
    The mountains stretch away.
Below, the maple masses sleep
    Where shore with water blends,
While midway on the tranquil deep
    The evening light descends.

So seemed it when yon hill's red crown,
    Of old, the Indian trod,
And, through the sunset air, looked down
    Upon the Smile of God.
To him of light and shade the laws
    No forest skeptic taught;
Their living and eternal Cause
    His truer instinct sought.

He saw these mountains in the light
    Which now across them shines;
This lake, in summer sunset bright,
    Walled round with sombering pines.
God near him seemed; from earth and skies

His loving voice he heard,
As, face to face, in Paradise,
Man stood before the Lord.

Thanks, O our Father! that, like him,
Thy tender love I see,
In radiant hill and woodland dim,
And tinted sunset sea.
For not in mockery dost Thou fill
Our earth with light and grace;
Thou hid'st no dark and cruel will
Behind Thy smiling face!

1850

It is doubtful that anyone's childhood was ever as thoroughly carefree as that of "The Barefoot Boy" portrayed here. Certainly Whittier's was not: after all, he exhausted his best energies—and his health—working on his father's farm. So how do we understand his claim to have been such a winsome "little man"? Do we simply dismiss the poem as nostalgia, that longing for a past that never was? A better strategy might be not to read the poem as a characterization of any individual's childhood. Instead, call it the celebration of a moment, a particular kind of moment hardly possible in adulthood, in which for a few eternal seconds or minutes or hours, all cares fall away, melting into a joy that stretches beyond time. Surely such a memory is worth a poem or two.

The Barefoot Boy

BLESSINGS on thee, little man,
Barefoot boy, with cheek of tan!
With thy turned-up pantaloons,
And thy merry whistled tunes;
With thy red lip, redder still
Kissed by strawberries on the hill;
With the sunshine on thy face,
Through thy torn brim's jaunty grace;
From my heart I give thee joy,—
I was once a barefoot boy!
Prince thou art,—the grown-up man
Only is republican.
Let the million-dollared ride!
Barefoot, trudging at his side,
Thou hast more than he can buy
In the reach of ear and eye,—
Outward sunshine, inward joy:
Blessings on thee, barefoot boy!

Oh for boyhood's painless play,
Sleep that wakes in laughing day,
Health that mocks the doctor's rules,
Knowledge never learned of schools,
Of the wild bee's morning chase,
Of the wild-flower's time and place,
Flight of fowl and habitude
Of the tenants of the wood;
How the tortoise bears his shell,
How the woodchuck digs his cell,
And the ground-mole sinks his well;
How the robin feeds her young,

75

How the oriole's nest is hung;
Where the whitest lilies blow,
Where the freshest berries grow,
Where the ground-nut trails its vine,
Where the wood-grape's clusters shine;
Of the black wasp's cunning way,
Mason of his walls of clay,
And the architectural plans
Of gray hornet artisans!
For, eschewing books and tasks,
Nature answers all he asks;
Hand in hand with her he walks,
Face to face with her he talks,
Part and parcel of her joy,—
Blessings on the barefoot boy!

Oh for boyhood's time of June,
Crowding years in one brief moon,
When all things I heard or saw,
Me, their master, waited for.
I was rich in flowers and trees,
Humming-birds and honey-bees;
For my sport the squirrel played,
Plied the snouted mole his spade;
For my taste the blackberry cone
Purpled over hedge and stone;
Laughed the brook for my delight
Through the day and through the night,
Whispering at the garden wall,
Talked with me from fall to fall;
Mine the sand-rimmed pickerel pond,
Mine the walnut slopes beyond,
Mine, on bending orchard trees,

Apples of Hesperides!
Still as my horizon grew,
Larger grew my riches too;
All the world I saw or knew
Seemed a complex Chinese toy,
Fashioned for a barefoot boy!

Oh for festal dainties spread,
Like my bowl of milk and bread;
Pewter spoon and bowl of wood,
On the door-stone, gray and rude!
O'er me, like a regal tent,
Cloudy-ribbed, the sunset bent,
Purple-curtained, fringed with gold,
Looped in many a wind-swung fold;
While for music came the play
Of the pied frogs' orchestra;
And, to light the noisy choir,
Lit the fly his lamp of fire.
I was monarch: pomp and joy
Waited on the barefoot boy!

Cheerily, then, my little man,
Live and laugh, as boyhood can!
Though the flinty slopes be hard,
Stubble-speared the new-mown sward,
Every morn shall lead thee through
Fresh baptisms of the dew;
Every evening from thy feet
Shall the cool wind kiss the heat:
All too soon these feet must hide
In the prison cells of pride,
Lose the freedom of the sod,
Like a colt's for work be shod,

Made to tread the mills of toil,
Up and down in ceaseless moil:
Happy if their track be found
Never on forbidden ground;
Happy if they sink not in
Quick and treacherous sands of sin.
Ah! that thou couldst know thy joy,
Ere it passes, barefoot boy!

1855

Whittier's biographer Roland Woodwell tells us that "The Last Walk in Autumn" was one of the poems in which Whittier felt real satisfaction. His pleasure may have been due to the fact that it was one of the few pieces in which he gave himself space to reflect upon those things that mattered most to him, with less concern than usual about arriving at all the correct preconceived answers. The result is a mature, revealing contemplation of his successes and of his personal and professional failures—a poem that carries not only the claim but the very ring of hard-won truth.

The Last Walk in Autumn

I

O'er the bare woods, whose outstretched hands
   Plead with the leaden heavens in vain,
I see, beyond the valley lands,
   The sea's long level dim with rain.

78

Around me all things, stark and dumb,
Seem praying for the snows to come,
And, for the summer bloom and greenness gone,
With winter's sunset lights and dazzling morn
     atone.

II

Along the river's summer walk,
    The withered tufts of asters nod;
And trembles on its arid stalk
    The hoar plume of the golden-rod.
And on a ground of sombre fir,
And azure-studded juniper,
The silver birch its buds of purple shows,
And scarlet berries tell where bloomed the sweet
    wild-rose!

III

With mingled sound of horns and bells,
    A far-heard clang, the wild geese fly,
Storm-sent, from Arctic moors and fells,
    Like a great arrow through the sky,
Two dusky lines converged in one,
Chasing the southward-flying sun;
While the brave snow-bird and the hardy jay
Call to them from the pines, as if to bid them stay.

IV

I passed this way a year ago:
    The wind blew south; the noon of day
Was warm as June's; and save that snow
    Flecked the low mountains far away,
And that the vernal-seeming breeze
Mocked faded grass and leafless trees,

I might have dreamed of summer as I lay,
Watching the fallen leaves with the soft wind at
        play.

V

Since then, the winter blasts have piled
        The white pagodas of the snow
On these rough slopes, and, strong and wild,
        Yon river, in its overflow
Of spring-time rain and sun, set free,
Crashed with its ices to the sea;
And over these gray fields, then green and gold,
The summer corn has waved, the thunder's organ
        rolled.

VI

Rich gift of God! A year of time!
        What pomp of rise and shut of day,
What hues wherewith our Northern clime
        Makes autumn's dropping woodlands gay,
What airs outblown from ferny dells,
And clover-bloom and sweetbrier smells,
What songs of brooks and birds, what fruits and
        flowers,
Green woods and moonlit snows, have in its round
        been ours!

VII

I know not how, in other lands,
        The changing seasons come and go;
What splendors fall on Syrian sands,
        What purple lights on Alpine snow!
Nor how the pomp of sunrise waits
On Venice at her watery gates;

A dream alone to me is Arno's vale,
And the Alhambra's halls are but a traveller's tale.

VIII
Yet, on life's current, he who drifts
  Is one with him who rows or sails;
And he who wanders widest lifts
  No more of beauty's jealous veils
Than he who from his doorway sees
The miracle of flowers and trees,
Feels the warm Orient in the noonday air,
And from cloud minarets hears the sunset call to
    prayer!

IX
The eye may well be glad that looks
  Where Pharpar's fountains rise and fall;
But he who sees his native brooks
  Laugh in the sun, has seen them all.
The marble palaces of Ind
Rise round him in the snow and wind;
From his lone sweetbrier Persian Hafiz smiles,
And Rome's cathedral awe is in his woodland
    aisles.

X
And thus it is my fancy blends
  The near at hand and far and rare;
And while the same horizon bends
  Above the silver-sprinkled hair
Which flashed the light of morning skies
On childhood's wonder-lifted eyes,
Within its round of sea and sky and field,
Earth wheels with all her zones, the Kosmos stands
    revealed.

XI

And thus the sick man on his bed,
    The toiler to his task-work bound,
Behold their prison-walls outspread,
    Their clipped horizon widen round!
While freedom-giving fancy waits,
Like Peter's angel at the gates,
The power is theirs to baffle care and pain,
To bring the lost world back, and make it theirs
        again!

XII

What lack of goodly company,
    When masters of the ancient lyre
Obey my call, and trace for me
    Their words of mingled tears and fire!
I talk with Bacon, grave and wise,
I read the world with Pascal's eyes;
And priest and sage, with solemn brows austere,
And poets, garland-bound, the Lords of Thought,
        draw near.

XIII

Methinks, O friend, I hear thee say,
    "In vain the human heart we mock;
Bring living guests who love the day,
    Not ghosts who fly at crow of cock!
The herbs we share with flesh and blood
Are better than ambrosial food
With laurelled shades." I grant it, nothing loath,
But doubly blest is he who can partake of both.

XIV

He who might Plato's banquet grace,
    Have I not seen before me sit,
And watched his puritanic face,
    With more than Eastern wisdom lit?
Shrewd mystic! who, upon the back
Of his Poor Richard's Almanac
Writing the Sufi's song, the Gentoo's dream,
Links Manu's age of thought to Fulton's age of
    steam!

XV

Here too, of answering love secure,
    Have I not welcomed to my hearth
The gentle pilgrim troubadour,
    Whose songs have girdled half the earth;
Whose pages, like the magic mat
Whereon the Eastern lover sat,
Have borne me over Rhine-land's purple vines,
And Nubia's tawny sands, and Phrygia's mountain
    pines!

XVI

And he, who to the lettered wealth
    Of ages adds the lore unpriced,
The wisdom and the moral health,
    The ethics of the school of Christ;
The statesman to his holy trust,
As the Athenian archon, just,
Struck down, exiled like him for truth alone,
Has he not graced my home with beauty all his
    own?

XVII

What greetings smile, what farewells wave,
　　What loved ones enter and depart!
The good, the beautiful, the brave,
　　The Heaven-lent treasures of the heart!
How conscious seems the frozen sod
And beechen slope whereon they trod!
The oak-leaves rustle, and the dry grass bends
Beneath the shadowy feet of lost or absent friends.

XVIII

Then ask not why to these bleak hills
　　I cling, as clings the tufted moss,
To bear the winter's lingering chills,
　　The mocking spring's perpetual loss.
I dream of lands where summer smiles,
And soft winds blow from spicy isles,
But scarce would Ceylon's breath of flowers be
　　　　sweet,
Could I not feel thy soil, New England, at my feet!

XIX

At times I long for gentler skies,
　　And bathe in dreams of softer air,
But homesick tears would fill the eyes
　　That saw the Cross without the Bear.
The pine must whisper to the palm,
The north-wind break the tropic calm;
And with the dreamy languor of the Line,
The North's keen virtue blend, and strength to
　　　　beauty join.

XX

Better to stem with heart and hand
    The roaring tide of life, than lie,
Unmindful, on its flowery strand,
    Of God's occasions drifting by!
Better with naked nerve to bear
The needles of this goading air,
Than, in the lap of sensual ease, forego
The godlike power to do, the godlike aim to know.

XXI

Home of my heart! to me more fair
    Than gay Versailles or Windsor's halls,
The painted, shingly town-house where
    The freeman's vote for Freedom falls!
The simple roof where prayer is made,
Than Gothic groin and colonnade;
The living temple of the heart of man,
Than Rome's sky-mocking vault, or many-spired
    Milan!

XXII

More dear thy equal village schools,
    Where rich and poor the Bible read,
Than classic halls where Priestcraft rules,
    And Learning wears the chains of Creed;
Thy glad Thanksgiving, gathering in
The scattered sheaves of home and kin,
Than the mad license ushering Lenten pains,
Or holidays of slaves who laugh and dance in
    chains.

XXIII

And sweet homes nestle in these dales,
    And perch along these wooded swells;
And, blest beyond Arcadian vales,
    They hear the sound of Sabbath bells!
Here dwells no perfect man sublime,
Nor woman winged before her time,
But with the faults and follies of the race,
Old home-bred virtues hold their not unhonored
    place.

XXIV

Here manhood struggles for the sake
    Of mother, sister, daughter, wife,
The graces and the loves which make
    The music of the march of life;
And woman, in her daily round
Of duty, walks on holy ground.
No unpaid menial tills the soil, nor here
Is the bad lesson learned at human rights to sneer.

XXV

Then let the icy north-wind blow
    The trumpets of the coming storm,
To arrowy sleet and blinding snow
    Yon slanting lines of rain transform.
Young hearts shall hail the drifted cold,
    As gayly as I did of old;
And I; who watch them through the frosty pane,
Unenvious, live in them my boyhood o'er again.

XXVI

And I will trust that He who heeds
      The life that hides in mead and wold,
Who hangs yon alder's crimson beads,
      And stains these mosses green and gold,
Will still, as He hath done, incline
His gracious care to me and mine;
Grant what we ask aright, from wrong debar,
And, as the earth grows dark, make brighter every
            star!

XXVII

I have not seen, I may not see,
      My hopes for man take form in fact,
But God will give the victory
      In due time; in that faith I act.
And he who sees the future sure,
The baffling present may endure,
And bless, meanwhile, the unseen Hand that leads
The heart's desires beyond the halting step of
            deeds.

XXVIII

And thou, my song, I send thee forth,
      Where harsher songs of mine have flown;
Go, find a place at home and hearth
      Where'er thy singer's name is known;
Revive for him the kindly thought
Of friends; and they who love him not,
Touched by some strain of thine, perchance may
            take
The hand he proffers all, and thank him for thy
            sake.

1857

Although this poem turns abruptly pedantic in its last eight stanzas, it is well worth reading for the dreary picture it paints of an old time burying-ground, a place with "scanty grace from Nature's hand / and none from that of art." Still more compelling than the image of that "windy wall of mossy stone" where the "stag-horn sumach grows," though, is what the choice suggests about the people who made it. What thoughts were in the minds of those good folks who chose the "dreariest spot in all the land," then "with a love as deep as ours /... left their dead with God"?

The Old Burying-Ground

Our vales are sweet with fern and rose,
   Our hills are maple-crowned;
But not from them our fathers chose
   The village burying-ground.

The dreariest spot in all the land
   To Death they set apart;
With scanty grace from Nature's hand,
   And none from that of art.

A winding wall of mossy stone,
   Frost-flung and broken, lines
A lonesome acre thinly grown
   With grass and wandering vines.

Without the wall a birch-tree shows
    Its drooped and tasselled head;
Within, a stag-horn sumach grows,
    Fern-leafed, with spikes of red.

There, sheep that graze the neighboring plain
    Like white ghosts come and go,
The farm-horse drags his fetlock chain,
    The cow-bell tinkles slow.

Low moans the river from its bed,
    The distant pines reply;
Like mourners shrinking from the dead,
    They stand apart and sigh.

Unshaded smites the summer sun,
    Unchecked the winter blast;
The school-girl learns the place to shun,
    With glances backward cast.

For thus our fathers testified,
    That he might read who ran,
The emptiness of human pride,
    The nothingness of man.

They dared not plant the grave with flowers,
    Nor dress the funeral sod,
Where, with a love as deep as ours,
    They left their dead with God.

The hard and thorny path they kept
    From beauty turned aside;
Nor missed they over those who slept
    The grace to life denied.

Yet still the wilding flowers would blow,
    The golden leaves would fall,
The seasons come, the seasons go,
    And God be good to all.

Above the graves the blackberry hung
    In bloom and green its wreath,
And harebells swung as if they rung
    The chimes of peace beneath.

The beauty Nature loves to share,
    The gifts she hath for all,
The common light, the common air,
    O'ercrept the graveyard's wall.

It knew the glow of eventide,
    The sunrise and the noon,
And glorified and sanctified
    It slept beneath the moon.

With flowers or snow-flakes for its sod,
    Around the seasons ran,
And evermore the love of God
    Rebuked the fear of man.

We dwell with fears on either hand
    Within a daily strife,
And spectral problems waiting stand
    Before the gates of life.

The doubts we vainly seek to solve,
    The truths we know, are one;
The known and nameless stars revolve
    Around the Central Sun.

And if we reap as we have sown,
    And take the dole we deal,
The law of pain is love alone,
    The wounding is to heal.

Unharmed from change to change we glide
    We fall as in our dreams;
The far-off terror at our side
    A smiling angel seems.

Secure on God's all-tender heart
    Alike rest great and small;
Why fear to lose our little part,
    When He is pledged for all?

O fearful heart and troubled brain!
    Take hope and strength from this,—
That Nature never hints in vain,
    Nor prophesies amiss.

Her wild birds sing the same sweet stave,
    Her lights and airs are given
Alike to playground and the grave;
    And over both is Heaven.

1858

From his youth Whittier was fascinated with folk tales and customs. His very first book was entitled *Legends of New England*, and his passion for the old ways endured throughout his life. Nothing in his earlier work, however, compares with the masterful combination of legend and art that resulted in "Telling the Bees." Starting with a folk practice, Whittier crafted a moving lyric about the death of a young girl. It is exactly the kind of subject that Whittier—and most of his contemporaries—would normally have over-written into sentimentality. In this instance, though, Whittier manages to tell his tale in a dramatic first-person narrative, then stop.

Telling The Bees

A remarkable custom, brought from the Old Country, formerly prevailed in the rural districts of New England. On the death of a member of the family, the bees were at once informed of the event, and their hives dressed in mourning. This ceremonial was supposed to be necessary to prevent the swarms from leaving their hives and seeking a new home.

HERE is the place; right over the hill
    Runs the path I took;
You can see the gap in the old wall still,
    And the stepping-stones in the shallow
        brook.

There is the house, with the gate red-barred,
   And the poplars tall;
And the barn's brown length, and the cattle
       yard,
   And the white horns tossing above the wall.

There are the beehives ranged in the sun;
   And down by the brink
Of the brook are her poor flowers, weed
       o'errun,
   Pansy and daffodil, rose and pink.

A year has gone, as the tortoise goes,
   Heavy and slow;
And the same rose blows, and the same sun
       glows,
   And the same brook sings of a year ago.

There's the same sweet clover-smell in the
       breeze;
   And the June sun warm
Tangles his wings of fire in the trees,
   Setting, as then, over Fernside farm.

I mind me how with a lover's care
   From my Sunday coat
I brushed off the burrs, and smoothed my hair,
   And cooled at the brookside my brow and
       throat.

Since we parted, a month had passed,—
   To love, a year;
Down through the beeches I looked at last
   On the little red gate and the well-sweep
       near.

I can see it all now,—the slantwise rain
  Of light through the leaves,
The sundown's blaze on her window-pane,
  The bloom of her roses under the eaves.

Just the same as a month before,—
  The house and the trees,
The barn's brown gable, the vine by the door,—
  Nothing changed but the hives of bees.

Before them, under the garden wall,
  Forward and back,
Went drearily singing the chore-girl small,
  Draping each hive with a shred of black.

Trembling, I listened: the summer sun
  Had the chill of snow;
For I knew she was telling the bees of one
  Gone on the journey we all must go!

Then I said to myself, "My Mary weeps
  For the dead to-day:
Haply her blind old grandsire sleeps
  The fret and the pain of his age away."

But her dog whined low; on the doorway sill,
  With his cane to his chin,
The old man sat; and the chore-girl still
  Sung to the bees stealing out and in.

And the song she was singing ever since
  In my ear sounds on:—
"Stay at home, pretty bees, fly not hence!
  Mistress Mary is dead and gone!"

1858

In "The Double-Headed Snake of Newbury," Whittier starts once again with a folk source, but this time contrives to spin a lighthearted lesson from the stuff of legend. The monsters that plagued the Puritan imagination do not plague Whittier's, and he can glean a little pleasure at Cotton Mather's expense. But we can also imagine the poet, a confirmed bachelor, taking a friendly jab or two at his married friends, possibly even pointing out, on some ripe occasion, that the amphisbaena seems to be flourishing well enough in Amesbury.

The Double-Headed Snake of Newbury

"Concerning ye Amphisbaena, as soon as I received your commands, I made diligent inquiry:… he assures me yᵗ it had really two heads, one at each end; two mouths, two stings or tongues."—Rev. Christopher Toppan *to* Cotton Mather.

Far away in the twilight time
Of every people, in every clime,
Dragons and griffins and monsters dire,
Born of water, and air, and fire,
Or nursed, like the Python, in the mud
And ooze of the old Deucalion flood,
Crawl and wriggle and foam with rage,
Through dusk tradition and ballad age.

So from the childhood of Newbury town
And its time of fable the tale comes down
Of a terror which haunted bush and brake,
The Amphisbaena, the Double Snake!

Thou who makest the tale thy mirth,
Consider that strip of Christian earth
On the desolate shore of a sailless sea,
Full of terror and mystery,
Half redeemed from the evil hold
Of the wood so dreary, and dark, and old,
Which drank with its lips of leaves the dew
When Time was young, and the world was
       new,
And wove its shadows with sun and moon,
Ere the stones of Cheops were squared and
       hewn.
Think of the sea's dread monotone,
Of the mournful wail from the pine-wood
       blown,
Of the strange, vast splendors that lit the
       North,
Of the troubled throes of the quaking earth,
And the dismal tales the Indian told,
Till the settler's heart at his hearth grew cold,
And he shrank from the tawny wizard boasts,
And the hovering shadows seemed full of
       ghosts,
And above, below, and on every side,
The fear of his creed seemed verified;—
And think, if his lot were now thine own,
To grope with terrors nor named nor known,
How laxer muscle and weaker nerve

And a feebler faith thy need might serve;
And own to thyself the wonder more
That the snake had two heads, and not a
      score!

Whether he lurked in the Oldtown fen
Or the gray earth-flax of the Devil's Den,
Or swam in the wooded Artichoke,
Or coiled by the Northman's Written Rock,
Nothing on record is left to show;
Only the fact that he lived, we know,
And left the cast of a double head
In the scaly mask which he yearly shed.
For he carried a head where his tail should be,
And the two, of course, could never agree,
But wriggled about with main and might,
Now to the left and now to the right;
Pulling and twisting this way and that,
Neither knew what the other was at.

A snake with two heads, lurking so near!
Judge of the wonder, guess at the fear!
Think what ancient gossips might say,
Shaking their heads in their dreary way,
Between the meetings on Sabbath-day!
How urchins, searching at day's decline
The Common Pasture for sheep or kine,
The terrible double-ganger heard
In leafy rustle or whir of bird!
Think what a zest it gave to the sport,
In berry-time, of the younger sort,
As over pastures blackberry-twined,
Reuben and Dorothy lagged behind,

And closer and closer, for fear of harm,
The maiden clung to her lover's arm;
And how the spark, who was forced to stay,
By his sweetheart's fears, till the break of day,
Thanked the snake for the fond delay!

Far and wide the tale was told,
Like a snowball growing while it rolled.
The nurse hushed with it the baby's cry;
And it served, in the worthy minister's eye,
To paint the primitive serpent by.
Cotton Mather came galloping down
All the way to Newbury town,
With his eyes agog and his ears set wide,
And his marvellous inkhorn at his side;
Stirring the while in the shallow pool
Of his brains for the lore he learned at school,
To garnish the story, with here a streak
Of Latin and there another of Greek:
And the tales he heard and the notes he took,
Behold! are they not in his Wonder-Book?

Stories, like dragons, are hard to kill.
If the snake does not, the tale runs still
In Byfield Meadows, on Pipestave Hill.
And still, whenever husband and wife
Publish the shame of their daily strife,
And, with mad cross-purpose, tug and strain
At either end of the marriage-chain,
The gossips say with a knowing shake
Of their gray heads, "Look at the Double Snake!
One in body and two in will,
The Amphisbaena is living still!"

                                        1859

"My Playmate" is a more typical sentimental handling of the lost girl theme, but it nevertheless achieves an excellence of its own. Though Whittier himself doubted the worth of this bit of "pastoral song," as he called it, he chose to submit it for publication anyway, as was his custom, and let his editor and readers be judge and jury. What may be more surprising than Whittier's choice is the fact that, once published, it was considered, by no less an artist than Alfred Lord Tennyson, to be a "perfect poem." Its quality is at least in part due to the thoughtful combinations of images that bring together the lofty and the rustic, all in the context of loving remembrance. Good readers cannot overlook, for example, the "jewelled hands" and "silken gown" of heaven, in vivid contrast with "the homespun lap wherein / I shook the walnuts down."

My Playmate

THE pines were dark on Ramoth hill,
  Their song was soft and low;
The blossoms in the sweet May wind
  Were falling like the snow.

The blossoms drifted at our feet,
  The orchard birds sang clear;
The sweetest and the saddest day
  It seemed of all the year.

For, more to me than birds or flowers,
    My playmate left her home,
And took with her the laughing spring,
    The music and the bloom.

She kissed the lips of kith and kin,
    She laid her hand in mine:
What more could ask the bashful boy
    Who fed her father's kine?

She left us in the bloom of May:
    The constant years told o'er
Their seasons with as sweet May morns,
    But she came back no more.

I walk, with noiseless feet, the round
    Of uneventful years;
Still o'er and o'er I sow the spring
    And reap the autumn ears.

She lives where all the golden year
    Her summer roses blow;
The dusky children of the sun
    Before her come and go.

There haply with her jewelled hands
    She smooths her silken gown,—
No more the homespun lap wherein
    I shook the walnuts down.

The wild grapes wait us by the brook,
    The brown nuts on the hill,
And still the May-day flowers make sweet
    The woods of Follymill.

The lilies blossom in the pond,
  The bird builds in the tree,
The dark pines sing on Ramoth hill
  The slow song of the sea.

I wonder if she thinks of them,
  And how the old time seems,—
If ever the pines of Ramoth wood
  Are sounding in her dreams.

I see her face, I hear her voice;
  Does she remember mine?
And what to her is now the boy
  Who fed her father's kine?

What cares she that the orioles build
  For other eyes than ours,—
That other hands with nuts are filled,
  And other laps with flowers?

O playmate in the golden time!
  Our mossy seat is green,
Its fringing violets blossom yet,
  The old trees o'er it lean.

The winds so sweet with birch and fern
  A sweeter memory blow;
And there in spring the veeries sing
  The song of long ago.

And still the pines of Ramoth wood
  Are moaning like the sea,—
The moaning of the sea of change
  Between myself and thee!

                                        1860

The poet begins his view of "Monadnock from Wachuset" by exclaiming, "I would I were a painter, for the sake / Of a sweet picture..." and indeed this portrait of a New England mountain farmscape is one of his best. But as the piece progresses, the brilliance of nature slips to the background, and the focus falls instead on an admiring speculation about the old woman who "lived and died here in the peace of God!" As a result, there is a creative tension between the poem's stated purpose and its actual effect. The poet and his companion, Elizabeth Lloyd Howell, reflect that such a woman must have been more noble even than the beauty of the place, her "inward life" more praiseworthy than "Nature's raiment"—however resplendent.

Monadnock From Wachuset

I would I were a painter, for the sake
   Of a sweet picture, and of her who led,
     A fitting guide, with reverential tread,
Into that mountain mystery. First a lake
   Tinted with sunset; next the wavy lines
      Of far receding hills; and yet more far,
   Monadnock lifting from his night of pines
     His rosy forehead to the evening star.
Beside us, purple-zoned, Wachuset laid
His head against the West, whose warm light made
     His aureole; and o'er him, sharp and clear,
Like a shaft of lightning in mid-launching stayed,

A single level cloud-line, shone upon
By the fierce glances of the sunken sun,
    Menaced the darkness with its golden
        spear!

So twilight deepened round us. Still and black
The great woods climbed the mountain at our
        back;
And on their skirts, where yet the lingering day
On the shorn greenness of the clearing lay,
    The brown old farm-house like a bird's-nest
        hung.
With home-life sounds the desert air was stirred:
The bleat of sheep along the hill we heard,
The bucket plashing in the cool, sweet well,
The pasture-bars that clattered as they fell;
Dogs barked, fowls fluttered, cattle lowed; the gate
Of the barn-yard creaked beneath the merry
        weight
    Of sun-brown children, listening, while they
        swung,
        The welcome sound of supper-call to hear;
        And down the shadowy lane, in tinklings
        clear,
    The pastoral curfew of the cow-bell rung.
Thus soothed and pleased, our backward path we
        took,
Praising the farmer's home. He only spake,
Looking into the sunset o'er the lake,
    Like one to whom the far-off is most near:
"Yes, most folks think it has a pleasant look;
    I love it for my good old mother's sake,
        Who lived and died here in the peace of
        God!"

The lesson of his words we pondered o'er,
As silently we turned the eastern flank
Of the mountain, where its shadow deepest sank,
Doubling the night along our rugged road:
We felt that man was more than his abode,—
    The inward life than Nature's raiment more;
And the warm sky, the sundown-tinted hill,
    The forest and the lake, seemed dwarfed and
            dim
Before the saintly soul, whose human will
    Meekly in the Eternal footsteps trod,
Making her homely toil and household ways
An earthly echo of the song of praise
    Swelling from angel lips and harps of seraphim.

1862

All working poets occasionally break from their most comfortable forms to vary their versifying, and Whittier is no exception. Though rhyming verse was his mainstay, he was a great admirer of Milton—both as a man and as a poet—and in "Prelude" he adopts Milton's favored form of poetry, blank verse. More compelling than the formal change, however, is the change of theme and tone toward a realistic portrayal of rural poverty. If "Monadnock From Wachuset" celebrated a woman whose virtue overshadowed even the mountain vistas, this poem presents the opposite: a view of human life far less admirable than its setting. Though the lens of time seems often to have softened Whittier's views of pastoral yesterdays, here it is clear that the poet knew the underside of rural life—the desperation of physical and spiritual poverty and the degradation which could result. This theme, a rare one in Whittier's poetry, is handled no less deftly for its infrequency, is in fact as powerful as it is rare. The poet is brutally accurate in portraying "old homesteads, where no flower / Told that the spring had come"—and in communicating all that that sad fact implies.

Prelude to *Among the Hills*

ALONG the roadside, like the flowers of gold
That tawny Incas for their gardens wrought,
Heavy with sunshine droops the golden-rod,
And the red pennons of the cardinal-flowers
Hang motionless upon their upright staves.
The sky is hot and hazy, and the wind,
Wing-weary with its long flight from the south,
Unfelt; yet, closely scanned, yon maple leaf
With faintest motion, as one stirs in dreams,
Confesses it. The locust by the wall
Stabs the noon-silence with his sharp alarm.
A single hay-cart down the dusty road
Creaks slowly, with its driver fast asleep
On the load's top. Against the neighboring hill,
Huddled along the stone wall's shady side,
The sheep show white, as if a snowdrift still
Defied the dog-star. Through the open door
A drowsy smell of flowers—gray heliotrope,
And white sweet clover, and shy mignonette—
Comes faintly in, and silent chorus lends
To the pervading symphony of peace.

No time is this for hands long over-worn
To task their strength: and (unto Him be praise
Who giveth quietness!) the stress and strain
Of years that did the work of centuries
Have ceased, and we can draw our breath once more
Freely and full. So, as yon harvesters
Make glad their nooning underneath the elms
With tale and riddle and old snatch of song,
I lay aside grave themes, and idly turn
The leaves of memory's sketch-book, dreaming o'er
Old summer pictures of the quiet hills,
And human life, as quiet, at their feet.

And yet not idly all. A farmer's son,
Proud of field-lore and harvest craft, and feeling
All their fine possibilities, how rich
And restful even poverty and toil
Become when beauty, harmony, and love
Sit at their humble hearth as angels sat
At evening in the patriarch's tent, when man
Makes labor noble, and his farmer's frock
The symbol of a Christian chivalry
Tender and just and generous to her
Who clothes with grace all duty; still, I know
Too well the picture has another side,—
How wearily the grind of toil goes on
Where love is wanting, how the eye and ear
And heart are starved amidst the plenitude
Of nature, and how hard and colorless
Is life without an atmosphere. I look
Across the lapse of half a century,
And call to mind old homesteads, where no flower
Told that the spring had come, but evil weeds,
Nightshade and rough-leaved burdock in the place

Of the sweet doorway greeting of the rose
And honeysuckle, where the house walls seemed
Blistering in sun, without a tree or vine
To cast the tremulous shadow of its leaves
Across the curtainless windows, from whose panes
Fluttered the signal rags of shiftlessness.
Within, the cluttered kitchen floor, unwashed
(Broom-clean I think they called it); the best room
Stifling with cellar damp, shut from the air
In hot midsummer, bookless, pictureless
Save the inevitable sampler hung
Over the fireplace, or a mourning piece,
A green-haired woman, peony-cheeked, beneath
Impossible willows; the wide-throated hearth
Bristling with faded pine-boughs half concealing
The piled-up rubbish at the chimney's back;
And, in sad keeping with all things about them,
Shrill, querulous women, sour and sullen men,
Untidy, loveless, old before their time,
With scarce a human interest save their own
Monotonous round of small economies,
Or the poor scandal of the neighborhood;
Blind to the beauty everywhere revealed,
Treading the May-flowers with regardless feet;
For them the song-sparrow and the bobolink
Sang not, nor winds made music in the leaves;
For them in vain October's holocaust
Burned, gold and crimson, over all the hills,
The sacramental mystery of the woods.
Church-goers, fearful of the unseen Powers,
But grumbling over pulpit-tax and pew-rent,
Saving, as shrewd economists, their souls
And winter pork with the least possible outlay

Of salt and sanctity; in daily life
Showing as little actual comprehension
Of Christian charity and love and duty,
As if the Sermon on the Mount had been
Outdated like a last year's almanac:
Rich in broad woodlands and in half-tilled fields,
And yet so pinched and bare and comfortless,
The veriest straggler limping on his rounds,
The sun and air his sole inheritance,
Laughed at a poverty that paid its taxes,
And hugged his rags in self-complacency!

Not such should be the homesteads of a land
Where whoso wisely wills and acts may dwell
As king and lawgiver, in broad-acred state,
With beauty, art, taste, culture, books, to make
His hour of leisure richer than a life
Of fourscore to the barons of old time,
Our yeoman should be equal to his home
Set in the fair, green valleys, purple walled,
A man to match his mountains, not to creep
Dwarfed and abased below them. I would fain
In this light way (of which I needs must own
With the knife-grinder of whom Canning sings,
"Story, God bless you! I have none to tell you!")
Invite the eye to see and heart to feel
The beauty and the joy within their reach,—
Home, and home loves, and the beatitudes
Of nature free to all. Haply in years
That wait to take the places of our own,
Heard where some breezy balcony looks down
On happy homes, or where the lake in the moon
Sleeps dreaming of the mountains, fair as Ruth,

In the old Hebrew pastoral, at the feet
Of Boaz, even this simple lay of mine
May seem the burden of a prophecy,
Finding its late fulfilment in a change
Slow as the oak's growth, lifting manhood up
Through broader culture, finer manners, love,
And reverence, to the level of the hills.

O Golden Age, whose light is of the dawn,
And not of sunset, forward, not behind,
Flood the new heavens and earth, and with thee
      bring
All the old virtues, whatsoever things
Are pure and honest and of good repute,
But add thereto whatever bard has sung
Or seer has told of when in trance and dream
They saw the Happy Isles of prophecy!
Let Justice hold her scale, and Truth divide
Between the right and wrong; but give the heart
The freedom of its fair inheritance;
Let the poor prisoner, cramped and starved so long,
At Nature's table feast his ear and eye
With joy and wonder; let all harmonies
Of sound, form, color, motion, wait upon
The princely guest, whether in soft attire
Of leisure clad, or the coarse frock of toil,
And, lending life to the dead form of faith,
Give human nature reverence for the sake
Of One who bore it, making it divine
With the ineffable tenderness of God;
Let common need, the brotherhood of prayer,
The heirship of an unknown destiny,
The unsolved mystery round about us, make

A man more precious than the gold of Ophir.
Sacred, inviolate, unto whom all things
Should minister, as outward types and signs
Of the eternal beauty which fulfils
The one great purpose of creation, Love,
The sole necessity of Earth and Heaven!

1869

R ead as a reflection of nineteenth-century
gender roles—or even of old-fashioned educational practices—"In School Days" is a little
unsettling. But if we forgive the poet his era (as we
hope he forgives us ours) and hear what the poem
says about innocence and love and self-sacrifice,
something within it strikes at our core. After all,
how many people do you know who would "lament their triumph" if it meant your loss?

Such a simple but sincere expression of affection continues to touch us, just as it touched
Whittier's contemporaries—including Henry
Wadsworth Longfellow. Eight years after the poem
had been published, that poet wrote to a friend,
"Certainly there is more in education than is set
down in the school books. Whittier has touched
this point very poetically in that little lyric of his
called 'In School Days.'"

In School-Days

STILL sits the school-house by the road,
  A ragged beggar sleeping;
Around it still the sumachs grow,
  And blackberry-vines are creeping.

Within, the master's desk is seen,
  Deep scarred by raps official;
The warping floor, the battered seats,
  The jack-knife's carved initial;

The charcoal frescos on its wall;
  Its door's worn sill, betraying
The feet that, creeping slow to school,
  Went storming out to playing!

Long years ago a winter sun
  Shone over it at setting;
Lit up its western window-panes,
  And low eaves' icy fretting.

It touched the tangled golden curls,
  And brown eyes full of grieving,
Of one who still her steps delayed
  When all the school were leaving.

For near her stood the little boy
  Her childish favor singled:
His cap pulled low upon a face
  Where pride and shame were mingled

Pushing with restless feet the snow
  To right and left, he lingered;—
As restlessly her tiny hands
  The blue-checked apron fingered.

He saw her lift her eyes; he felt
  The soft hand's light caressing,
And heard the tremble of her voice,
  As if a fault confessing.

"I'm sorry that I spelt the word:
  I hate to go above you,
Because,"—the brown eyes lower fell,—
  "Because, you see, I love you!"

Still memory to a gray-haired man
  That sweet child-face is showing.
Dear girl! the grasses on her grave
  Have forty years been growing!

He lives to learn, in life's hard school,
  How few who pass above him
Lament their triumph and his loss,
  Like her,—because they love him.

1870

Though Whittier tries to give "My Birthday" a lighter cast, it never quite recovers from its powerfully dark opening: "Beneath the moonlight

and the snow / Lies dead my latest year." Almost
by reflex, he shifts his attention to the goodness of
life that remains, but that anticipation seems
overshadowed by a more powerful emotion: the
fear of lacking purpose, the fear that "he who
braved the polar frost / [may] Faint by the isles of
balm." Having served the cause of abolition much
of his life as a radical reformer—a writer, an editor,
a lobbyist, an organizer, even as an occasional
office-holder—it is little wonder that he feels
greater comfort in the "tumult of the truth" than in
the self-indulgence that may come with age and
easy circumstances. As the poem concludes, his
concerns become, in his most natural turn, a
prayer.

My Birthday

BENEATH the moonlight and the snow
  Lies dead my latest year;
The winter winds are wailing low
  Its dirges in my ear.

I grieve not with the moaning wind
  As if a loss befell;
Before me, even as behind,
  God is, and all is well!

His light shines on me from above,
  His low voice speaks within,—
The patience of immortal love
  Outwearying mortal sin.

Not mindless of the growing years
    Of care and loss and pain,
My eyes are wet with thankful tears
    For blessings which remain.

If dim the gold of life has grown,
    I will not count it dross,
Nor turn from treasures still my own
    To sigh for lack and loss.

The years no charm from Nature take;
    As sweet her voices call,
As beautiful her mornings break,
    As fair her evenings fall.

Love watches o'er my quiet ways,
    Kind voices speak my name,
And lips that find it hard to praise
    Are slow, at least, to blame.

How softly ebb the tides of will!
    How fields, once lost or won,
Now lie behind me green and still
    Beneath a level sun!

How hushed the hiss of party hate,
    The clamor of the throng!
How old, harsh voices of debate
    Flow into rhythmic song!

Methinks the spirit's temper grows
    Too soft in this still air;
Somewhat the restful heart foregoes
    Of needed watch and prayer.

The bark by tempest vainly tossed
   May founder in the calm,
And he who braved the polar frost
   Faint by the isles of balm.

Better than self-indulgent years
   The outflung heart of youth,
Than pleasant songs in idle ears
   The tumult of the truth.

Rest for the weary hands is good,
   And love for hearts that pine,
But let the manly habitude
   Of upright souls be mine.

Let winds that blow from heaven refresh,
   Dear Lord, the languid air;
And let the weakness of the flesh
   Thy strength of spirit share.

And, if the eye must fail of light,
   The ear forget to hear,
Make clearer still the spirit's sight,
   More fine the inward ear!

Be near me in mine hours of need
   To soothe, or cheer, or warn,
And down these slopes of sunset lead
   As up the hills of morn!

                               1871

Some literary critics, uneasy perhaps with the poet's religious devotion, have argued that Whittier simply couldn't write a decent poem about nature without some religious interjection. And it is true that in the lens with which he viewed the world, the spiritual seldom drifted too far out of focus. But that was the core of the man. Put plainly, feelings of intense joy in the presence of beauty naturally turned the poet's mind heavenward, and his poems simply testify to that turning. For Whittier, "common earth" was truly nothing less than "a holy ground."

A Summer Pilgrimage

To kneel before some saintly shrine,
To breathe the health of airs divine,
Or bathe where sacred rivers flow,
The cowled and turbaned pilgrims go.
I too, a palmer, take, as they
With staff and scallop-shell, my way
To feel, from burdening cares and ills,
The strong uplifting of the hills.

The years are many since, at first,
For dreamed-of wonders all athirst,
I saw on Winnipesaukee fall
The shadow of the mountain wall.
Ah! where are they who sailed with me

The beautiful island-studded sea?
And am I he whose keen surprise
Flashed out from such unclouded eyes?

Still, when the sun of summer burns,
My longing for the hills returns;
And northward, leaving at my back
The warm vale of the Merrimac,
I go to meet the winds of morn,
Blown down the hill-gaps, mountain-born,
Breathe scent of pines, and satisfy
The hunger of a lowland eye.

Again I see the day decline
Along a ridged horizon line;
Touching the hill-tops, as a nun
Her beaded rosary, sinks the sun.
One lake lies golden, which shall soon
Be silver in the rising moon;
And one, the crimson of the skies
And mountain purple multiplies.

With the untroubled quiet blends
The distance-softened voice of friends;
The girl's light laugh no discord brings
To the low song the pine-tree sings;
And, not unwelcome, comes the hail
Of boyhood from his nearing sail.
The human presence breaks no spell,
And sunset still is miracle!

Calm as the hour, methinks I feel
A sense of worship o'er me steal;

Not that of satyr-charming Pan,
No cult of Nature shaming man,
Not Beauty's self, but that which lives
And shines through all the veils it weaves,—
Soul of the mountain, lake, and wood,
Their witness to the Eternal Good!

And if, by fond illusion, here
The earth to heaven seems drawing near,
And yon outlying range invites
To other and serener heights,
Scarce hid behind its topmost swell,
The shining Mounts Delectable!
A dream may hint of truth no less
Than the sharp light of wakefulness.

As through her veil of incense smoke
Of old the spell-rapt priestess spoke,
More than her heathen oracle,
May not this trance of sunset tell
That Nature's forms of loveliness
Their heavenly archetypes confess,
Fashioned like Israel's ark alone
From patterns in the Mount made known?

A holier beauty overbroods
These fair and faint similitudes;
Yet not unblest is he who sees
Shadows of God's realities,
And knows beyond this masquerade
Of shape and color, light and shade,
And dawn and set, and wax and wane,
Eternal verities remain.

O gems of sapphire, granite set!
O hills that charmed horizons fret!
I know how fair your morns can break,
In rosy light on isle and lake;
How over wooded slopes can run
The noonday play of cloud and sun,
And evening droop her oriflamme
Of gold and red in still Asquam.

The summer moons may round again,
And careless feet these hills profane;
These sunsets waste on vacant eyes
The lavish splendor of the skies;
Fashion and folly, misplaced here,
Sigh for their natural atmosphere,
And travelled pride the outlook scorn
Of lesser heights than Matterhorn:

But let me dream that hill and sky
Of unseen beauty prophesy;
And in these tinted lakes behold
The trailing of the raiment fold
Of that which, still eluding gaze,
Allures to upward-tending ways,
Whose footprints make, wherever found,
Our common earth a holy ground.

1883

In "Sweet Fern," the beauty of nature serves as a bridge not into religious reverie but into a memory of romance. The scent of the fern recalls to the poet's mind a vision of a girl who "plucked a fern" and "smiling, held it up, / While from her hand the wild, sweet scent / I drank as from a cup."

Sweet Fern

THE subtle power in perfume found
 Nor priest nor sibyl vainly learned;
On Grecian shrine or Aztec mound
 No censer idly burned.

That power the old-time worships knew,
 The Corybantes' frenzied dance,
The Pythian priestess swooning through
 The wonderland of trance.

And Nature holds, in wood and field,
 Her thousand sunlit censers still;
To spells of flower and shrub we yield
 Against or with our will.

I climbed a hill path strange and new
 With slow feet, pausing at each turn;
A sudden waft of west wind blew
 The breath of the sweet fern.

That fragrance from my vision swept
   The alien landscape; in its stead,
Up fairer hills of youth I stepped,
   As light of heart as tread.

I saw my boyhood's lakelet shine
   Once more through rifts of woodland shade;
I knew my river's winding line
   By morning mist betrayed.

With me June's freshness, lapsing brook,
   Murmurs of leaf and bee, the call
Of birds, and one in voice and look
   In keeping with them all.

A fern beside the way we went
   She plucked, and, smiling, held it up,
While from her hand the wild, sweet scent
   I drank as from a cup.

O potent witchery of smell!
   The dust-dry leaves to life return,
And she who plucked them owns the spell
   And lifts her ghostly fern.

Or sense or spirit? Who shall say
   What touch the chord of memory thrills?
It passed, and left the August day
   Ablaze on lonely hills.

1886

III.
Snow-Bound:
A Winter Idyll

In 1865, Whittier began *Snow-Bound*. His intention was less to give his generation a piece of art than to give his greatest treasure—his memories of his family and boyhood—to his niece, Lizzie. He wanted her to know the place and the people that had created the household he had shared with her father. By the next year, the riches of the poem already extended far beyond the family hearth. Looking back, we can see that this poem presented the poet's disillusioned countrymen, weary with civil war and newly urban, just the view of the past they wanted and needed. In response, they made him rich. Not only did sales from the first edition bring him ten thousand dollars (about twenty times his income in 1865)—it created such a demand for his work that he was able to name his own price when submitting material to magazines. For the first time, he could live on the income generated by his poetry.

The poem's reception by twentieth-century scholars and critics, as might be expected, has been mixed, but remains positive. Some scholars have gone so far as to claim that the poem presents our finest record of a particular stage of American farm life. Others would suggest that it is no more an accurate view of farm life than the "Barefoot Boy" is a view of childhood. Ultimately any reservations are less important than this single fact: it presents an image which has become a significant part of how we, like its original readers, envision early nineteenth-century rural life. And thus it remains a part of the American mind.

In spite of the radical revaluations of American literary scholarship, *Snow-Bound* seems destined to hold its place in the first rank. It is significant that this poem was written when Whittier had been a productive writer for nearly forty years. Now approaching 60 and a journeyman versifier, he could not have been better prepared. And he had at last come upon the single great topic that would allow him the range and situation to use all the themes which he could manipulate most skillfully. His boyhood, his religious conscience, the pleasures of home, the wonders of nature–each would be considered in the mellow glow of a warming fire, the softening light of memory.

Snow-Bound: A Winter Idyll

TO THE MEMORY OF THE HOUSEHOLD IT DESCRIBES
THIS POEM IS DEDICATED BY THE AUTHOR

The inmates of the family at the Whittier homestead who are referred to in the poem were my father, mother, my brother and two sisters, and my uncle and aunt, both unmarried. In addition, there was the district school master, who boarded with us. The "not unfeared, half-welcome guest" was Harriet Livermore, daughter of Judge Livermore, of New Hampshire, a young woman of fine natural ability, enthusiastic, eccentric, with slight control over her violent temper, which sometimes made her religious profession doubtful. She was equally ready to exhort in school-house prayer-meetings and dance in a Washington ball-room, while her father was a member of congress. She early embraced the doctrine of the Second Advent, and felt it her duty to proclaim the Lord's speedy coming. With this message she crossed the Atlantic and spent the greater part of a long life in travelling over Europe and Asia. She lived some time with Lady Hester Stanhope, a woman as fantastic and mentally strained as herself, on the slope of Mt. Lebanon, but finally quarrelled with her in regard to two white horses with red marks on their backs which suggested the idea of saddles, on which her titled hostess expected to ride into Jerusalem with the Lord. A friend of mine found her, when quite an old woman, wandering in Syria with a tribe of Arabs, who with the Oriental notion that madness is inspiration, accepted her as their prophetess and leader. At the time referred to in *Snow-Bound* she was boarding at the Rocks Village, about two miles from us.

In my boyhood, in our lonely farm-house, we had scanty sources of information; few books and only a small weekly newspaper. Our only annual was the *Almanac*. Under such circumstances story-telling was a necessary resource in the long winter evenings. My father when a young man had traversed the wilderness to Canada, and could tell us of his adventures with Indians and wild beasts, and of his sojourn in the French villages. My uncle was ready with his record of hunting and fishing and, it must be confessed, with stories which he at least half believed, of witchcraft and apparitions. My mother, who was born in the Indian-haunted region of Somersworth, New Hampshire, between Dover and Portsmouth, told us of the inroads of the savages, and the narrow escape of her ances-tors. She described strange people who lived on the Piscataqua and Cocheco, among whom was

Bantam the sorcerer. I have in my possession the
wizard's "conjuring book," which he solemnly
opened when consulted. It is a copy of Cornelius
Agrippa's *Magic*, printed in 1651, dedicated to Dr.
Robert Child, who, like Michael Scott, had learned
    "the art of glammorie
    In Padua beyond the sea,"
and who is famous in the annals of Massachusetts,
where he was at one time a resident, as the first
man who dared petition the General Court for
liberty of conscience. The full title of the book is
*Three Books of Occult Philosophy, by Henry Cornelius
Agrippa, Knight, Doctor of both Laws, Counsellor to
Caesar's Sacred Majesty and Judge of the Prerogative
Court.*

    "As the Spirits of Darkness be stronger in the dark, so
Good Spirits, which be Angels of Light, are augmented
not only by the Divine light of the Sun, but also by our
common Wood Fire: and as the Celestial Fire drives
away dark spirits, so also this our Fire of Wood doth the
same."—COR. AGRIPPA, *Occult Philosophy*, Book I. ch v.

    "Announced by all the trumpets of the sky,
    Arrives the snow, and, driving o'er the fields,
    Seems nowhere to alight: the whited air
    Hides hills and woods, the river and the heaven,
    And veils the farm-house at the garden's end.
    The sled and traveller stopped, the courier's feet
    Delayed, all friends shut out, the housemates sit
    Around the radiant fireplace, enclosed
    In a tumultuous privacy of storm."
              EMERSON. "The Snow Storm."

THE sun that brief December day
Rose cheerless over hills of gray,
And, darkly circled, gave at noon
A sadder light than waning moon.
Slow tracing down the thickening sky

128

Its mute and ominous prophecy,
A portent seeming less than threat,
It sank from sight before it set.
A chill no coat, however stout,
Of homespun stuff could quite shut out,
A hard, dull bitterness of cold,
That checked, mid-vein, the circling race
Of life-blood in the sharpened face,
The coming of the snow-storm told.
The wind blew east; we heard the roar
Of Ocean on his wintry shore,
And felt the strong pulse throbbing there
Beat with low rhythm our inland air.

Meanwhile we did our nightly chores,—
Brought in the wood from out of doors,
Littered the stalls, and from the mows
Raked down the herd's-grass for the cows:
Heard the horse whinnying for his corn;
And, sharply clashing horn on horn,
Impatient down the stanchion rows
The cattle shake their walnut bows;
While, peering from his early perch
Upon the scaffold's pole of birch,
The cock his crested helmet bent
And down his querulous challenge sent.

Unwarmed by any sunset light
The gray day darkened into night,
A night made hoary with the swarm
And whirl-dance of the blinding storm,
As zigzag, wavering to and fro,
Crossed and recrossed the wingèd snow:
And ere the early bedtime came

The white drift piled the window-frame,
And through the glass the clothes-line posts
Looked in like tall and sheeted ghosts.

So all night long the storm roared on:
The morning broke without a sun;
In tiny spherule traced with lines
Of Nature's geometric signs,
In starry flake, and pellicle,
All day the hoary meteor fell;
And, when the second morning shone,
We looked upon a world unknown,
On nothing we could call our own.
Around the glistening wonder bent
The blue walls of the firmament,
No cloud above, no earth below,—
A universe of sky and snow!
The old familiar sights of ours
Took marvellous shapes; strange domes and
          towers
Rose up where sty or corn-crib stood,
Or garden-wall, or belt of wood;
A smooth white mound the brush-pile
          showed,
A fenceless drift what once was road;
The bridle-post an old man sat
With loose-flung coat and high cocked hat;
The well-curb had a Chinese roof;
And even the long sweep, high aloof,
In its slant splendor, seemed to tell
Of Pisa's leaning miracle.

A prompt, decisive man, no breath
Our father wasted: "Boys, a path!"

Well pleased, (for when did farmer boy
Count such a summons less than joy?)
Our buskins on our feet we drew;
With mittened hands, and caps drawn low,
To guard our necks and ears from snow,
We cut the solid whiteness through.
And, where the drift was deepest, made
A tunnel walled and overlaid
With dazzling crystal: we had read
Of rare Aladdin's wondrous cave,
And to our own his name we gave,
With many a wish the luck were ours
To test his lamp's supernal powers.
We reached the barn with merry din,
And roused the prisoned brutes within.
The old horse thrust his long head out,
And grave with wonder gazed about;
The cock his lusty greeting said,
And forth his speckled harem led;
The oxen lashed their tails, and hooked,
And mild reproach of hunger looked;
The hornëd patriarch of the sheep,
Like Egypt's Amun roused from sleep,
Shook his sage head with gesture mute,
And emphasized with stamp of foot.

All day the gusty north-wind bore
The loosening drift its breath before;
Low circling round its southern zone,
The sun through dazzling snow-mist shone.
No church-bell lent its Christian tone
To the savage air, no social smoke
Curled over woods of snow-hung oak.
A solitude made more intense

By dreary-voicëd elements,
The shrieking of the mindless wind,
The moaning tree-boughs swaying blind,
And on the glass the unmeaning beat
Of ghostly finger-tips of sleet.
Beyond the circle of our hearth
No welcome sound of toil or mirth
Unbound the spell, and testified
Of human life and thought outside.
We minded that the sharpest ear
The buried brooklet could not hear,
The music of whose liquid lip
Had been to us companionship,
And, in our lonely life, had grown
To have an almost human tone.

As night drew on, and, from the crest
Of wooded knolls that ridged the west,
The sun, a snow-blown traveller, sank
From sight beneath the smothering bank,
We piled, with care, our nightly stack
Of wood against the chimney-back,—
The oaken log, green, huge, and thick,
And on its top the stout back-stick;
The knotty forestick laid apart,
And filled between with curious art
The ragged brush; then, hovering near,
We watched the first red blaze appear,
Heard the sharp crackle, caught the gleam
On whitewashed wall and sagging beam,
Until the old, rude-furnished room
Burst, flower-like, into rosy bloom;
While radiant with a mimic flame
Outside the sparkling drift became,

And through the bare-boughed lilac-tree
Our own warm hearth seemed blazing free.
The crane and pendent trammels showed,
The Turks' heads on the andirons glowed;
While childish fancy, prompt to tell
The meaning of the miracle,
Whispered the old rhyme: *"Under the tree,*
When fire outdoors burns merrily,
There the witches are making tea."

The moon above the eastern wood
Shone at its full; the hill-range stood
Transfigured in the silver flood,
Its blown snows flashing cold and keen,
Dead white, save where some sharp ravine
Took shadow, or the sombre green
Of hemlocks turned to pitchy black
Against the whiteness at their back.
For such a world and such a night
Most fitting that unwarming light,
Which only seemed where'er it fell
To make the coldness visible.

Shut in from all the world without,
We sat the clean-winged hearth about,
Content to let the north-wind roar
In baffled rage at pane and door,
While the red logs before us beat
The frost-line back with tropic heat;
And ever, when a louder blast
Shook beam and rafter as it passed,
The merrier up its roaring draught
The great throat of the chimney laughed;
The house-dog on his paws outspread

Laid to the fire his drowsy head,
The cat's dark silhouette on the wall
A couchant tiger's seemed to fall;
And, for the winter fireside meet,
Between the andirons' straddling feet,
The mug of cider simmered slow,
The apples sputtered in a row,
And, close at hand, the basket stood
With nuts from brown October's wood.

What matter how the night behaved?
What matter how the north-wind raved?
Blow high, blow low, not all its snow
Could quench our hearth-fire's ruddy glow.
O Time and Change!—with hair as gray
As was my sire's that winter day,
How strange it seems, with so much gone
Of life and love, to still live on!
Ah, brother! only I and thou
Are left of all that circle now,—
The dear home faces whereupon
That fitful firelight paled and shone.
Henceforward, listen as we will,
The voices of that hearth are still;
Look where we may, the wide earth o'er,
Those lighted faces smile no more.
We tread the paths their feet have worn,
    We sit beneath their orchard trees,
    We hear, like them, the hum of bees
And rustle of the bladed corn;
We turn the pages that they read,
    Their written words we linger o'er,
But in the sun they cast no shade,
No voice is heard, no sign is made,

No step is on the conscious floor!
Yet Love will dream, and Faith will trust,
(Since He who knows our need is just,)
That somehow, somewhere, meet we must.
Alas for him who never sees
The stars shine through his cypress-trees!
Who, hopeless, lays his dead away,
Nor looks to see the breaking day
Across the mournful marbles play!
Who hath not learned, in hours of faith,
    The truth to flesh and sense unknown,
That Life is ever lord of Death,
    And Love can never lose its own!

We sped the time with stories old,
Wrought puzzles out, and riddles told,
Or stammered from our school-book lore
"The Chief of Gambia's golden shore."
How often since, when all the land
Was clay in Slavery's shaping hand,
As if a far-blown trumpet stirred
The languorous sin-sick air, I heard:
"Does not the voice of reason cry,
    Claim the first right which Nature gave,
From the red scourge of bondage fly,
    Nor deign to live a burdened slave!"
Our father rode again his ride
On Memphremagog's wooded side;
Sat down again to moose and samp
In trapper's hut and Indian camp;
Lived o'er the old idyllic ease
Beneath St. François' hemlock-trees;
Again for him the moonlight shone
On Norman cap and bodiced zone;

Again he heard the violin play
Which led the village dance away.
And mingled in its merry whirl
The grandam and the laughing girl.
Or, nearer home, our steps he led
Where Salisbury's level marshes spread
    Mile-wide as flies the laden bee;
Where merry mowers, hale and strong,
Swept, scythe on scythe, their swaths along
    The low green prairies of the sea.
We shared the fishing off Boar's Head,
    And round the rocky Isles of Shoals
    The hake-broil on the drift-wood coals;
The chowder on the sand-beach made,
Dipped by the hungry, steaming hot,
With spoons of clam-shell from the pot.
We heard the tales of witchcraft old,
And dream and sign and marvel told
To sleepy listeners as they lay
Stretched idly on the salted hay,
Adrift along the winding shores,
When favoring breezes deigned to blow
The square sail of the gundelow
And idle lay the useless oars.

Our mother, while she turned her wheel
Or run the new-knit stocking-heel,
Told how the Indian hordes came down
At midnight on Cocheco town,
And how her own great-uncle bore
His cruel scalp-mark to fourscore.
Recalling, in her fitting phrase,
    So rich and picturesque and free,
    (The common unrhymed poetry

Of simple life and country ways,)
The story of her early days,—
She made us welcome to her home;
Old hearths grew wide to give us room;
We stole with her a frightened look
At the gray wizard's conjuring-book,
The fame whereof went far and wide
Through all the simple country side;
We heard the hawks at twilight play,
The boat-horn on Piscataqua,
The loon's weird laughter far away;
We fished her little trout-brook, knew
What flowers in wood and meadow grew,
What sunny hillsides autumn-brown
She climbed to shake the ripe nuts down,
Saw where in sheltered cove and bay
The ducks' black squadron anchored lay,
And heard the wild-geese calling loud
Beneath the gray November cloud.

Then, haply, with a look more grave,
And soberer tone, some tale she gave
From painful Sewel's ancient tome,
Beloved in every Quaker home,
Of faith fire-winged by martyrdom,
Or Chalkley's Journal, old and quaint,—
Gentlest of skippers, rare sea-saint!—
Who, when the dreary calms prevailed,
And water-butt and bread-cask failed,
And cruel, hungry eyes pursued
His portly presence mad for food,
With dark hints muttered under breath
Of casting lots for life or death,
Offered, if Heaven withheld supplies,

To be himself the sacrifice.
Then, suddenly, as if to save
The good man from his living grave,
A ripple on the water grew,
A school of porpoise flashed in view.
"Take, eat," he said, "and be content;
These fishes in my stead are sent
By Him who gave the tangled ram
To spare the child of Abraham."

Our uncle, innocent of books,
Was rich in lore of fields and brooks,
The ancient teachers never dumb
Of Nature's unhoused lyceum.
In moons and tides and weather wise,
He read the clouds as prophecies,
And foul or fair could well divine,
By many an occult hint and sign,
Holding the cunning-warded keys
To all the woodcraft mysteries;
Himself to Nature's heart so near
That all her voices in his ear
Of beast or bird had meanings clear,
Like Apollonius of old,
Who knew the tales the sparrows told,
Or Hermes, who interpreted
What the sage cranes of Nilus said;
A simple, guileless, childlike man,
Content to live where life began;
Strong only on his native grounds,
The little world of sights and sounds
Whose girdle was the parish bounds,
Whereof his fondly partial pride
The common features magnified,

As Surrey hills to mountains grew
In White of Selborne's loving view,—
He told how teal and loon he shot,
And how the eagle's eggs he got,
The feats on pond and river done,
The prodigies of rod and gun;
Till, warming with the tales he told,
Forgotten was the outside cold,
The bitter wind unheeded blew,
From ripening corn the pigeons flew,
The partridge drummed i' the wood, the mink
Went fishing down the river-brink.
In fields with bean or clover gay,
The woodchuck, like a hermit gray,
    Peered from the doorway of his cell;
The muskrat plied the mason's trade,
And tier by tier his mud-walls laid;
And from the shagbark overhead
    The grizzled squirrel dropped his shell.

Next, the dear aunt, whose smile of cheer
And voice in dreams I see and hear,—
The sweetest woman ever Fate
Perverse denied a household mate,
Who, lonely, homeless, not the less
Found peace in love's unselfishness,
And welcome wheresoe'er she went,
A calm and gracious element,
Whose presence seemed the sweet income
And womanly atmosphere of home,—
Called up her girlhood memories,
The huskings and the apple-bees,
The sleigh-rides and the summer sails,
Weaving through all the poor details

And homespun warp of circumstance
A golden woof-thread of romance.
For well she kept her genial mood
And simple faith of maidenhood;
Before her still a cloud-land lay,
The mirage loomed across her way;
The morning dew, that dries so soon
With others, glistened at her noon;
Through years of toil and soil and care,
From glossy tress to thin gray hair,
All unprofaned she held apart
The virgin fancies of the heart.
Be shame to him of woman born
Who hath for such but thought of scorn.

There, too, our elder sister plied
Her evening task the stand beside;
A full, rich nature, free to trust,
Truthful and almost sternly just,
Impulsive, earnest, prompt to act,
And make her generous thought a fact,
Keeping with many a light disguise
The secret of self-sacrifice.
O heart sore-tried! thou hast the best
That Heaven itself could give thee,—rest,
Rest from all bitter thoughts and things!
How many a poor one's blessing went
With thee beneath the low green tent
Whose curtain never outward swings!

As one who held herself a part
Of all she saw, and let her heart
Against the household bosom lean,
Upon the motley-braided mat

Our youngest and our dearest sat,
Lifting her large, sweet, asking eyes,
   Now bathed in the unfading green
And holy peace of Paradise.
Oh, looking from some heavenly hill,
   Or from the shade of saintly palms,
   Or silver reach of river calms,
Do those large eyes behold me still?
With me one little year ago:—
The chill weight of the winter snow
   For months upon her grave has lain;
And now, when summer south-winds blow
   And brier and harebell bloom again,
I tread the pleasant paths we trod,
I see the violet-sprinkled sod
Whereon she leaned, too frail and weak
The hillside flowers she loved to seek,
Yet following me where'er I went
With dark eyes full of love's content.
The birds are glad; the brier-rose fills
The air with sweetness; all the hills
Stretch green to June's unclouded sky;
But still I wait with ear and eye
For something gone which should be nigh,
A loss in all familiar things,
In flower that blooms, and bird that sings.
And yet, dear heart! remembering thee,
   Am I not richer than of old?
Safe in thy immortality,
   What change can reach the wealth I hold ?
   What chance can mar the pearl and gold
Thy love hath left in trust with me?
And while in life's late afternoon,
   Where cool and long the shadows grow,

I walk to meet the night that soon
  Shall shape and shadow overflow,
I cannot feel that thou art far,
Since near at need the angels are;
And when the sunset gates unbar,
  Shall I not see thee waiting stand,
And, white against the evening star,
    The welcome of thy beckoning hand?

Brisk wielder of the birch and rule,
The master of the district school
Held at the fire his favored place,
Its warm glow lit a laughing face
Fresh-hued and fair, where scarce appeared
The uncertain prophecy of beard.
He teased the mitten-blinded cat,
Played cross-pins on my uncle's hat,
Sang songs, and told us what befalls
In classic Dartmouth's college halls.
Born the wild Northern hills among,
From whence his yeoman father wrung
By patient toil subsistence scant,
Not competence and yet not want,
He early gained the power to pay
His cheerful, self-reliant way;
Could doff at ease his scholar's gown
To peddle wares from town to town;
Or through the long vacation's reach
In lonely lowland districts teach,
Where all the droll experience found
At stranger hearths in boarding round,
The moonlit skater's keen delight,
The sleigh-drive through the frosty night,
The rustic party, with its rough

Accompaniment of blind-man's-buff,
And whirling-plate, and forfeits paid,
His winter task a pastime made.
Happy the snow-locked homes wherein
He tuned his merry violin,
Or played the athlete in the barn,
Or held the good dame's winding-yarn,
Or mirth-provoking versions told
Of classic legends rare and old,
Wherein the scenes of Greece and Rome
Had all the commonplace of home,
And little seemed at best the odds
'Twixt Yankee pedlers and old gods;
Where Pindus-born Arachthus took
The guise of any grist-mill brook,
And dread Olympus at his will
Became a huckleberry hill.

A careless boy that night he seemed;
     But at his desk he had the look
And air of one who wisely schemed,
     And hostage from the future took
     In trainëd thought and lore of book.
Large-brained, clear-eyed, of such as he
Shall Freedom's young apostles be,
Who, following in War's bloody trail,
Shall every lingering wrong assail;
All chains from limb and spirit strike,
Uplift the black and white alike;
Scatter before their swift advance
The darkness and the ignorance,
The pride, the lust, the squalid sloth,
Which nurtured Treason's monstrous growth,
Made murder pastime, and the hell

Of prison-torture possible;
The cruel lie of caste refute,
Old forms remould, and substitute
For Slavery's lash the freeman's will,
For blind routine, wise-handed skill;
A school-house plant on every hill,
Stretching in radiate nerve-lines thence
The quick wires of intelligence;
Till North and South together brought
Shall own the same electric thought,
In peace a common flag salute,
And, side by side in labor's free
And unresentful rivalry,
Harvest the fields wherein they fought.

Another guest that winter night
Flashed back from lustrous eyes the light.
Unmarked by time, and yet not young,
The honeyed music of her tongue
And words of meekness scarcely told
A nature passionate and bold,
Strong, self-concentred, spurning guide,
Its milder features dwarfed beside
Her unbent will's majestic pride.
She sat among us, at the best,
A not unfeared, half-welcome guest,
Rebuking with her cultured phrase
Our homeliness of words and ways.
A certain pard-like, treacherous grace
Swayed the lithe limbs and drooped the lash,
Lent the white teeth their dazzling flash;
And under low brows, black with night,
Rayed out at times a dangerous light;
The sharp heat-lightnings of her face

Presaging ill to him whom Fate
Condemned to share her love or hate.
A woman tropical, intense
In thought and act, in soul and sense,
She blended in a like degree
The vixen and the devotee,
Revealing with each freak or feint
  The temper of Petruchio's Kate,
The raptures of Siena's saint.
Her tapering hand and rounded wrist
Had facile power to form a fist;
The warm, dark languish of her eyes
Was never safe from wrath's surprise.
Brows saintly calm and lips devout
Knew every change of scowl and pout;
And the sweet voice had notes more high
And shrill for social battle-cry.

Since then what old cathedral town
Has missed her pilgrim staff and gown,
What convent-gate has held its lock
Against the challenge of her knock!
Through Smyrna's plague-hushed
        thoroughfares,
Up sea-set Malta's rocky stairs,
Gray olive slopes of hills that hem
Thy tombs and shrines, Jerusalem,
Or startling on her desert throne
The crazy Queen of Lebanon
With claims fantastic as her own,
Her tireless feet have held their way;
And still, unrestful, bowed, and gray,
She watches under Eastern skies,
  With hope each day renewed and fresh,

The Lord's quick coming in the flesh,
Whereof she dreams and prophesies!

Where'er her troubled path may be,
   The Lord's sweet pity with her go!
The outward wayward life we see,
   The hidden springs we may not know.
Nor is it given us to discern
   What threads the fatal sisters spun,
   Through what ancestral years has run
The sorrow with the woman born,
What forged her cruel chain of moods,
What set her feet in solitudes,
   And held the love within her mute,
What mingled madness in the blood,
   A life-long discord and annoy,
   Water of tears with oil of joy,
And hid within the folded bud
   Perversities of flower and fruit.
It is not ours to separate
The tangled skein of will and fate,
To show what metes and bounds should stand
Upon the soul's debatable land,
And between choice and Providence
Divide the circle of events;
But He who knows our frame is just,
Merciful and compassionate,
And full of sweet assurances
And hope for all the language is,
That He remembereth we are dust!

At last the great logs, crumbling low,
Sent out a dull and duller glow,
The bull's-eye watch that hung in view,

Ticking its weary circuit through,
Pointed with mutely warning sign
Its black hand to the hour of nine.
That sign the pleasant circle broke:
My uncle ceased his pipe to smoke,
Knocked from its bowl the refuse gray,
And laid it tenderly away;
Then roused himself to safely cover
The dull red brands with ashes over.
And while, with care, our mother laid
The work aside, her steps she stayed
One moment, seeking to express
Her grateful sense of happiness
For food and shelter, warmth and health,
And love's contentment more than wealth,
With simple wishes (not the weak,
Vain prayers which no fulfilment seek,
But such as warm the generous heart,
O'er-prompt to do with Heaven its part)
That none might lack, that bitter night,
For bread and clothing, warmth and light.

Within our beds awhile we heard
The wind that round the gables roared,
With now and then a ruder shock,
Which made our very bedsteads rock.
We heard the loosened clapboards tost,
The board-nails snapping in the frost;
And on us, through the unplastered wall,
Felt the light sifted snow-flakes fall.
But sleep stole on, as sleep will do
When hearts are light and life is new;
Faint and more faint the murmurs grew,

Till in the summer-land of dreams
They softened to the sound of streams,
Low stir of leaves, and dip of oars,
And lapsing waves on quiet shores.

Next morn we wakened with the shout
Of merry voices high and clear;
And saw the teamsters drawing near
To break the drifted highways out.
Down the long hillside treading slow
We saw the half-buried oxen go,
Shaking the snow from heads uptost,
Their straining nostrils white with frost.
Before our door the straggling train
Drew up, an added team to gain.
The elders threshed their hands a-cold,
    Passed, with the cider-mug, their jokes
    From lip to lip; the younger folks
Down the loose snow-banks, wrestling, rolled,
Then toiled again the cavalcade
    O'er windy hill, through clogged ravine,
    And woodland paths that wound between
Low drooping pine-boughs winter-weighed.
From every barn a team afoot,
At every house a new recruit,
Where, drawn by Nature's subtlest law,
Haply the watchful young men saw
Sweet doorway pictures of the curls
And curious eyes of merry girls,
Lifting their hands in mock defence
Against the snow-ball's compliments,
And reading in each missive tost
The charm with Eden never lost.

We heard once more the sleigh-bells' sound;
   And, following where the teamsters led,
The wise old Doctor went his round,
Just pausing at our door to say,
In the brief autocratic way
Of one who, prompt at Duty's call,
Was free to urge her claim on all,
   That some poor neighbor sick abed
At night our mother's aid would need.
For, one in generous thought and deed,
   What mattered in the sufferer's sight
   The Quaker matron's inward light,
The Doctor's mail of Calvin's creed?
All hearts confess the saints elect
   Who, twain in faith, in love agree,
And melt not in an acid sect
   The Christian pearl of charity!

So days went on: a week had passed
Since the great world was heard from last.
The Almanac we studied o'er,
Read and reread our little store
Of books and pamphlets, scarce a score;
One harmless novel, mostly hid
From younger eyes, a book forbid,
And poetry, (or good or bad,
A single book was all we had,)
Where Ellwood's meek, drab-skirted Muse,
   A stranger to the heathen Nine,
   Sang, with a somewhat nasal whine,
The wars of David and the Jews.
At last the floundering carrier bore
The village paper to our door.
Lo! broadening outward as we read,

To warmer zones the horizon spread
In panoramic length unrolled
We saw the marvels that it told.
Before us passed the painted Creeks,
   And daft McGregor on his raids
   In Costa Rica's everglades.
And up Taygetos winding slow
Rode Ypsilanti's Mainote Greeks,
A Turk's head at each saddle-bow!
Welcome to us its week-old news,
Its corner for the rustic Muse,
   Its monthly gauge of snow and rain,
Its record, mingling in a breath
The wedding bell and dirge of death:
Jest, anecdote, and love-lorn tale,
The latest culprit sent to jail;
Its hue and cry of stolen and lost,
Its vendue sales and goods at cost,
   And traffic calling loud for gain.
We felt the stir of hall and street,
The pulse of life that round us beat;
The chill embargo of the snow
Was melted in the genial glow;
Wide swung again our ice-locked door,
And all the world was ours once more!

Clasp, Angel of the backward look
   And folded wings of ashen gray
   And voice of echoes far away,
The brazen covers of thy book;
The weird palimpsest old and vast,
Wherein thou hid'st the spectral past;
Where, closely mingling, pale and glow
The characters of joy and woe;

The monographs of outlived years,
Or smile-illumed or dim with tears,
   Green hills of life that slope to death,
And haunts of home, whose vistaed trees
Shade off to mournful cypresses
   With the white amaranths underneath.
Even while I look, I can but heed
   The restless sands' incessant fall,
Importunate hours that hours succeed,
Each clamorous with its own sharp need,
   And duty keeping pace with all.
Shut down and clasp the heavy lids;
I hear again the voice that bids
The dreamer leave his dream midway
For larger hopes and graver fears:
Life greatens in these later years,
The century's aloe flowers to-day!

Yet, haply, in some lull of life,
Some Truce of God which breaks its strife,
The worldling's eyes shall gather dew,
   Dreaming in throngful city ways
Of winter joys his boyhood knew;
And dear and early friends—the few
Who yet remain—shall pause to view
   These Flemish pictures of old days;
Sit with me by the homestead hearth,
And stretch the hands of memory forth
   To warm them at the wood-fire's blaze!
And thanks untraced to lips unknown
Shall greet me like the odors blown
From unseen meadows newly mown,
Or lilies floating in some pond,

Wood-fringed, the wayside gaze beyond;
The traveller owns the grateful sense
Of sweetness near, he knows not whence,
And, pausing, takes with forehead bare
The benediction of the air.

1866

IV.
Crafting the Past

"Skipper Ireson's Ride"
and Other Stories

In addition to many poems of personal history, Whittier also excelled at casting the narratives of New England's history into verse romance. Given the hostilities of his vocation—as editor, lobbyist, and prophet-at-large—it must have been a relief for the poet to dwell at times on the past. From his boyhood, he loved the old tales of his region, the legends, the superstitions, even the real-life events as they began to turn the subtle shades of myth. So historical subjects were not only some of his first writings, but, during the maturity of his career, some of his most accomplished.

But here is a predicament: these long narratives are the most difficult kind of poetry for many contemporary readers to embrace. Human desires for excitement and adventure have not changed, but today readers seldom follow those particular desires down the trail of narrative verse. And why should they? Multi-billion dollar conglomerates compete to gratify the need for story with popular songs, television programs, and easy novels, so that there is hardly space left for what was once an extremely popular form.

Be that as it may, in his historical romances Whittier exercised not only some of his greatest craft, but demonstrated as well some of his most weighty interpersonal insight and religious understanding. Like all good literature, his best poems not only portray a particular event but reveal something about human nature as well. "How the Women Went From Dover" is as interesting for what it tells us about one brave citizen who met the priest "as man meets man" as it is for the adventure itself, and the women who accompany "Skipper Ireson's Ride" are as intriguing for what they don't do to the heartless captain—and why— as for what they do.

In the same way, it is the poet's psychological insight that rewards our reading of "The New Wife and the Old." Whittier was a master at spinning stories of straw into verses of gold, making romances perfectly good enough for the newspapers and popular magazines. But creating real poetry from legend was an achievement more rare. In this poem, he manages not simply to cast the events into meter and rhyme, but subtly to imply psychological truths about the relationships. One way or another, the ghost returns, the dead wife retrieves her ring, and the new wife is comforted. But then, the grievance of the ghost is not with her. Whittier perfects his art by suggesting the deeper pressures of the situation: for a moment, a window is opened on the brutality of the first marriage. The man whose strength is such a comfort to his new wife is revealed in all his weakness and former cruelty; he is haunted by one for whom "her early grave / Was as freedom to the slave."

The New Wife and the Old

The following ballad is founded upon one of the
marvellous legends connected with the famous
General M—, of Hampton, New Hampshire, who
was regarded by his neighbors as a Yankee Faust,
in league with the adversary. I give the story, as I
heard it when a child, from a venerable family
visitant.

Dark the halls, and cold the feast,
Gone the bridemaids, gone the priest.
All is over, all is done,
Twain of yesterday are one!
Blooming girl and manhood gray,
Autumn in the arms of May!

Hushed within and hushed without,
Dancing feet and wrestlers' shout;
Dies the bonfire on the hill;
All is dark and all is still,
Save the starlight, save the breeze
Moaning through the graveyard trees;
And the great sea-waves below,
Pulse of the midnight beating slow.

From the brief dream of a bride
She hath wakened, at his side.
With half-uttered shriek and start,—
Feels she not his beating heart?
And the pressure of his arm,
And his breathing near and warm?

Lightly from the bridal bed
Springs that fair dishevelled head,
And a feeling, new, intense,
Half of shame, half innocence,
Maiden fear and wonder speaks
Through her lips and changing cheeks.

From the oaken mantel glowing,
Faintest light the lamp is throwing
On the mirror's antique mould,
High-backed chair, and wainscot old,
And, through faded curtains stealing,
His dark sleeping face revealing.

Listless lies the strong man there,
Silver-streaked his careless hair;
Lips of love have left no trace
On that hard and haughty face;
And that forehead's knitted thought
Love's soft hand hath not unwrought.

"Yet," she sighs, "he loves me well,
More than these calm lips will tell.
Stooping to my lowly state,
He hath made me rich and great,
And I bless him, though he be
Hard and stern to all save me!"

While she speaketh; falls the light
O'er her fingers small and white;
Gold and gem, and costly ring
Back the timid lustre fling,—
Love's selectest gifts, and rare,
His proud hand had fastened there.

Gratefully she marks the glow
From those tapering lines of snow;
Fondly o'er the sleeper bending,
His black hair with golden blending,
In her soft and light caress,
Cheek and lip together press.

Ha!—that start of horror! why
That wild stare and wilder cry,
Full of terror, full of pain?
Is there madness in her brain?
Hark! that gasping, hoarse and low,
"Spare me,—spare me,—let me go!"

God have mercy!—icy cold
Spectral hands her own enfold,
Drawing silently from them
Love's fair gifts of gold and gem.
"Waken! save me!" still as death
At her side he slumbereth.

Ring and bracelet all are gone,
And that ice-cold hand withdrawn;
But she hears a murmur low,
Full of sweetness, full of woe,
Half a sigh and half a moan:
"Fear not! give the dead her own!"

Ah!—the dead wife's voice she knows!
That cold hand whose pressure froze,
Once in warmest life had borne
Gem and band her own hath worn.
"Wake thee! wake thee!" Lo, his eyes
Open with a dull surprise.

In his arms the strong man folds her,
Closer to his breast he holds her;
Trembling limbs his own are meeting,
And he feels her heart's quick beating:
"Nay, my dearest, why this fear?"
"Hush!" she saith, "the dead is here!"

"Nay, a dream,—an idle dream."
But before the lamp's pale gleam
Tremblingly her hand she raises.
There no more the diamond blazes,
Clasp of pearl, or ring of gold,—
"Ah!" she sighs, "her hand was cold!"

Broken words of cheer he saith,
But his dark lip quivereth,
And as o'er the past he thinketh,
From his young wife's arms he shrinketh;
Can those soft arms round him lie,
Underneath his dead wife's eye?

She her fair young head can rest
Soothed and childlike on his breast,
And in trustful innocence
Draw new strength and courage thence;
He, the proud man, feels within
But the cowardice of sin!

She can murmur in her thought
Simple prayers her mother taught,
And His blessed angels call,
Whose great love is over all;
He, alone, in prayerless pride,
Meets the dark Past at her side!

One, who living shrank with dread
From his look, or word, or tread,
Unto whom her early grave
Was as freedom to the slave
Moves him at this midnight hour,
With the dead's unconscious power!

Ah, the dead, the unforgot!
From their solemn homes of thought,
Where the cypress shadows blend
Darkly over foe and friend,
Or in love or sad rebuke,
Back upon the living look.

And the tenderest ones and weakest,
Who their wrongs have borne the meekest,
Lifting from those dark, still places,
Sweet and sad-remembered faces,
O'er the guilty hearts behind
An unwitting triumph find.

1843

If we want to read Maud Muller's tale as an easy romance and declare it foolish, we can certainly find reason to do so. The idyllic beauty of the setting and the apparent innocence of the characters lure us into just such an interpretation. Add to these elements the memorable and often quoted couplet, "For of all sad words of tongue or pen / The saddest are these: 'It might have been,'" and we can even catch ourselves lamenting, along with the misguided non-couple, that they'd gotten together.

But we misread the poem if we buy into the daydream. Whittier is more sophisticated than that. As sadly pretty as the story is, more careful reading reveals that the poem's moral attention is not on missed opportunity, but on an overactive sense of regret. The weakness the poet portrays is that all-too-human tendency to dream about impossibilities when we might better be dealing with reality.

Maud Muller

The recollection of some descendants of a Hessian deserter in the Revolutionary war bearing the name of Muller doubtless suggested the somewhat infelicitous title of a New England idyl. The poem had no real foundation in fact, though a hint of it may have been found in recalling an incident, trivial in itself, of a journey on the picturesque Maine seaboard with my sister some years before it was written. We had stopped to rest our tired horse under the shade of an apple-tree, and refresh him with water from a little brook which rippled through the stone wall across the road. A very beautiful young girl in scantest summer attire was at work in the hay-field, and as we talked with her we noticed that she strove to hide her bare feet by raking hay over them, blushing as she did so, through the tan of her cheek and neck.

MAUD MULLER on a summer's day
Raked the meadow sweet with hay.

Beneath her torn hat glowed the wealth
Of simple beauty and rustic health.

Singing, she wrought, and her merry glee
The mock-bird echoed from his tree.

But when she glanced to the far-off town,
White from its hill-slope looking down,

The sweet song died, and a vague unrest
And a nameless longing filled her breast,—

A wish that she hardly dared to own,
For something better than she had known.

The Judge rode slowly down the lane,
Smoothing his horse's chestnut mane.

He drew his bridle in the shade
Of the apple-trees, to greet the maid,

And asked a draught from the spring that
        flowed
Through the meadow across the road.

She stooped where the cool spring bubbled up,
And filled for him her small tin cup,

And blushed as she gave it, looking down
On her feet so bare, and her tattered gown.

"Thanks!" said the Judge; "a sweeter draught
From a fairer hand was never quaffed."

He spoke of the grass and flowers and trees,
Of the singing birds and the humming bees;

Then talked of the haying, and wondered
        whether
The cloud in the west would bring foul
        weather.

And Maud forgot her brier-torn gown,
And her graceful ankles bare and brown;

And listened, while a pleased surprise
Looked from her long-lashed hazel eyes.

At last, like one who for delay
Seeks a vain excuse, he rode away.

Maud Muller looked and sighed: "Ah me!
That I the Judge's bride might be!

"He would dress me up in silks so fine,
And praise and toast me at his wine.

"My father should wear a broadcloth coat,
My brother should sail a painted boat.

"I'd dress my mother so grand and gay,
And the baby should have a new toy each day.

"And I'd feed the hungry and clothe the poor,
And all should bless me who left our door."

The Judge looked back as he climbed the hill,
And saw Maud Muller standing still.

"A form more fair, a face more sweet,
Ne'er hath it been my lot to meet.

"And her modest answer and graceful air
Show her wise and good as she is fair.

"Would she were mine, and I to-day,
Like her, a harvester of hay;

"No doubtful balance of rights and wrongs,
Nor weary lawyers with endless tongues,

"But low of cattle and song of birds,
And health and quiet and loving words."

But he thought of his sisters, proud and cold,
And his mother, vain of her rank and gold.

So, closing his heart, the Judge rode on,
And Maud was left in the field alone.

But the lawyers smiled that afternoon,
When he hummed in court an old love-tune;

And the young girl mused beside the well
Till the rain on the unraked clover fell.

He wedded a wife of richest dower,
Who lived for fashion, as he for power.

Yet oft, in his marble hearth's bright glow,
He watched a picture come and go;

And sweet Maud Muller's hazel eyes
Looked out in their innocent surprise.

Oft, when the wine in his glass was red,
He longed for the wayside well instead;

And closed his eyes on his garnished rooms
To dream of meadows and clover-blooms.

And the proud man sighed, with a secret pain,
"Ah, that I were free again!

"Free as when I rode that day,
Where the barefoot maiden raked her hay."

She wedded a man unlearned and poor,
And many children played round her door.

But care and sorrow, and childbirth pain,
Left their traces on heart and brain.

And oft, when the summer sun shone hot
On the new-mown hay in the meadow lot,

And she heard the little spring brook fall
Over the roadside, through the wall,

In the shade of the apple-tree again
She saw a rider draw his rein;

And, gazing down with timid grace,
She felt his pleased eyes read her face.

Sometimes her narrow kitchen walls
Stretched away into stately halls;

The weary wheel to a spinnet turned,
The tallow candle an astral burned,

And for him who sat by the chimney lug,
Dozing and grumbling o'er pipe and mug,

A manly form at her side she saw,
And joy was duty and love was law.

Then she took up her burden of life again,
Saying only, "It might have been."

Alas for maiden, alas for Judge,
For rich repiner and household drudge!

God pity them both! and pity us all,
Who vainly the dreams of youth recall.

For of all sad words of tongue or pen,
The saddest are these: "It might have been!"

Ah, well! for us all some sweet hope lies
Deeply buried from human eyes;

And, in the hereafter, angels may
Roll the stone from its grave away!

                                        1854

At first glance Mary Garvin seems to be a pleasant but unlikely interweaving of legend and soap opera. Yet captivity tales on the American frontier were common enough—and not uncommonly true. What sets this story apart is the theological tension in which Whittier situates the adventure. As was often the case in such tales, contrasting cultures are at the center of the intrigue, but here the primary conflict is not between Native Americans and Euro-Americans but between French Catholics and New England Protestants. Much of the poem, while celebrating the triumph of physical and spiritual beauty over the "elders, grave and doubting," becomes a narrative argument against the narrowness of creedal religion. Granted, some critics might argue that this is a romance spoiled by a theological conclusion, but such a claim ignores the very center of Whittier's being: that deeply religious core that came to inform all of his mature work. The theme of this poem—and one of the central strands of Whittier's world-view—is well summed up in the line, "Creed and rite perchance may differ, yet our faith and hope be one."

Mary Garvin

FROM the heart of Waumbek Methna, from the
lake that never fails,

168

Falls the Saco in the green lap of Conway's
    intervales;
There, in wild and virgin freshness, its waters
    foam and flow,
As when Darby Field first saw them, two
    hundred years ago.

But, vexed in all its seaward course with
    bridges, dams, and mills,
How changed is Saco's stream, how lost its
    freedom of the hills,
Since travelled Jocelyn, factor Vines, and
    stately Champernoon
Heard on its banks the gray wolf's howl, the
    trumpet of the loon!

With smoking axle hot with speed, with
    steeds of fire and steam,
Wide-waked To-day leaves Yesterday behind
    him like a dream.
Still, from the hurrying train of Life, fly
    backward far and fast
The milestones of the fathers, the landmarks
    of the past.

But human hearts remain unchanged: the
    sorrow and the sin,
The loves and hopes and fears of old, are to
    our own akin;
And if, in tales our fathers told, the songs our
    mothers sung,
Tradition wears a snowy beard, Romance is
    always young.

169

O sharp-lined man of traffic, on Saco's banks
      to-day!
O mill-girl watching late and long the shuttle's
      restless play!
Let, for the once, a listening ear the working
      hand beguile,
And lend my old Provincial tale, as suits, a
      tear or smile!

The evening gun had sounded from gray Fort
      Mary's walls;
Through the forest, like a wild beast, roared
      and plunged the Saco's falls.

And westward on the sea-wind, that damp
      and gusty grew,
Over cedars darkening inland the smokes of
      Spurwink blew.

On the hearth of Farmer Garvin, blazed the
      crackling walnut log;
Right and left sat dame and goodman, and
      between them lay the dog,

Head on paws, and tail slow wagging, and
      beside him on her mat,
Sitting drowsy in the firelight, winked and
      purred the mottled cat.

"Twenty years!" said Goodman Garvin,
      speaking sadly, under breath,

And his gray head slowly shaking, as one who
      speaks of death.

The goodwife dropped her needles: "It is
      twenty years to-day,
Since the Indians fell on Saco, and stole our
      child away."

Then they sank into the silence, for each
      knew the other's thought,
Of a great and common sorrow, and words
      were needed not.

"Who knocks?" cried Goodman Garvin. The
      door was open thrown;
On two strangers, man and maiden, cloaked
      and furred, the firelight shone.

One with courteous gesture lifted the bearskin
      from his head;
"Lives here Elkanah Garvin?" "I am he,"the
      goodman said.

"Sit ye down, and dry and warm ye, for the
      night is chill with rain."
And the goodwife drew the settle, and stirred
      the fire amain.

The maid unclasped her cloak-hood, the
      firelight glistened fair
In her large, moist eyes, and over soft folds of
      dark brown hair.

Dame Garvin looked upon her: "It is Mary's
    self I see!
Dear heart!" she cried, "now tell me, has my
    child come back to me?"

"My name indeed is Mary," said the stranger
    sobbing wild;
"Will you be to me a mother? I am Mary
    Garvin's child!

"She sleeps by wooded Simcoe, but on her
    dying day
She bade my father take me to her kinsfolk
    far away.

"And when the priest besought her to do me
    no such wrong,
She said, 'May God forgive me! I have closed
    my heart too long.

" 'When I hid me from my father, and shut
    out my mother's call,
I sinned against those dear ones, and the
    Father of us all.

" 'Christ's love rebukes no home-love, breaks
    no tie of kin apart;
Better heresy in doctrine, than heresy of
    heart.

" ' Tell me not the Church must censure: she
    who wept the Cross beside

Never made her own flesh strangers, nor the
    claims of blood denied;

" 'And if she who wronged her parents, with
    her child atones to them,
Earthly daughter, Heavenly Mother! thou at
    least wilt not condemn!'

"So, upon her death-bed lying, my blessed
    mother spake;
As we come to do her bidding, so receive us
    for her sake."

"God be praised!" said Goodwife Garvin, "He
    taketh, and He gives;
He woundeth, but He healeth; in her child
    our daughter lives!"

"Amen!" the old man answered, as he
    brushed a tear away,
And, kneeling by his hearthstone, said, with
    reverence, "Let us pray."

All its Oriental symbols, and its Hebrew
    paraphrase,
Warm with earnest life and feeling, rose his
    prayer of love and praise.

But he started at beholding, as he rose from
    off his knee,
The stranger cross his forehead with the sign
    of Papistrie.

"What is this?" cried Farmer Garvin. "Is an
      English Christian's home
A chapel or a mass-house, that you make the
      sign of Rome?"

Then the young girl knelt beside him, kissed
      his trembling hand, and cried:
"Oh, forbear to chide my father; in that faith
      my mother died!

"On her wooden cross at Simcoe the dews and
      sunshine fall,
As they fall on Spurwink's graveyard; and the
      dear God watches all!"

The old man stroked the fair head that rested
      on his knee;
"Your words, dear child," he answered, "are
      God's rebuke to me.

"Creed and rite perchance may differ, yet our
      faith and hope be one.
Let me be your father's father, let him be to
      me a son."

When the horn, on Sabbath morning,through
      the still and frosty air,
From Spurwink, Pool, and Black Point,called
      to sermon and to prayer,

To the goodly house of worship, where, in
      order due and fit,

As by public vote directed, classed and ranked
    the people sit;

Mistress first and goodwife after, clerkly squire
    before the clown,
From the brave coat, lace-embroidered, to the
    gray frock, shading down;

From the pulpit read the preacher, "Goodman
    Garvin and his wife
Fain would thank the Lord, whose kindness
    as followed them through life,

"For the great and crowning mercy, that their
    daughter, from the wild,
Where she rests (they hope in God's peace),
    has sent to them her child;

"And the prayers of all God's people they ask,
    that they may prove
Not unworthy, through their weakness, of
    such special proof of love."

As the preacher prayed, uprising, the aged
    couple stood,
And the fair Canadian also, in her modest
    maidenhood.

Thought the elders, grave and doubting, "She
    is Papist born and bred";
Thought the young men, " 'T is an angel in
    Mary Garvin's stead!"

                        1856

Although Skipper Ireson's story of vengeance and contrition was related to Whittier by a fellow schoolmate at Haverhill Academy, thirty years passed before he succeeded in changing the events into verse. When the poem happened at last, the result was Whittier's best ballad on an historical theme. While the version of the story Whittier was told—and which he passes on to us—is, as he admits in his note, not quite true, it does tell Truth. That said, the poem stands as a superb piece of artistic transformation. What begins as a rollicking tale of revenge becomes believable and poignant as Ireson himself realizes the inward source of his true punishment—"What is the shame that clothes the skin / To the nameless horror that lives within?" How fitting then, too, that the women's just wrath is changed to a dark mercy.

Skipper Ireson's Ride

In the valuable and carefully prepared *History of Marblehead*, published in 1879 by Samuel Roads, Jr., it is stated that the crew of Captain Ireson, rather than himself, were responsible for the abandonment of the disabled vessel. To screen themselves they charged their captain with the crime. In view of this the writer of the ballad addressed the following letter to the historian:—

OAK KNOLL, DANVERS, 5 *mo.* 18, 1880.
MY DEAR FRIEND; I heartily thank thee for a copy of thy *History of Marblehead*. I have read it with

great interest and think good use has been made of the abundant material. No town in Essex County has a record more honorable than Marblehead; no one has done more to develop the industrial interests of our New England seaboard, and certainly none have given such evidence of self-sacrificing patriotism. I am glad the story of it has been at last told, and told so well. I have now no doubt that thy version of Skipper Ireson's ride is the correct one. My verse was founded solely on a fragment of rhyme which I heard from one of my early schoolmates, a native of Marblehead.

I supposed the story to which it referred dated back at least a century. I knew nothing of the participators, and the narrative of the ballad was pure fancy. I am glad for the sake of truth and justice that the real facts are given in thy book. I certainly would not knowingly do injustice to any one, dead or living.

I am very truly thy friend,
John G. Whittier

OF all the rides since the birth of time,
Told in story or sung in rhyme,—
On Apuleius's Golden Ass,
Or one-eyed Calender's horse of brass,
Witch astride of a human back,
Islam's prophet on Al-Borák,—
The strangest ride that ever was sped
Was Ireson's, out from Marblehead!
Old Floyd Ireson, for his hard heart,
Tarred and feathered and carried in a cart
By the women of Marblehead!

Body of turkey, head of owl,
Wings a-droop like a rained-on fowl,
Feathered and ruffled in every part,

177

Skipper Ireson stood in the cart.
Scores of women, old and young,
Strong of muscle, and glib of tongue,
Pushed and pulled up the rocky lane,
Shouting and singing the shrill refrain:
    "Here's Flud Oirson, fur his horrd horrt,
    Torr'd an' futherr'd an' corr'd in a corrt
    By the women o' Morble'ead!"

Wrinkled scolds with hands on hips,
Girls in bloom of cheek and lips,
Wild-eyed, free-limbed, such as chase
Bacchus round some antique vase,
Brief of skirt, with ankles bare,
Loose of kerchief and loose of hair,
With conch-shells blowing and fish-horns'
                twang,
Over and over the Maenads sang:
    "Here's Flud Oirson, fur his horrd horrt,
    Torr'd an' futherr'd an' corr'd in a corrt
    By the women o' Morble'ead!"

Small pity for him!—He sailed away
From a leaking ship in Chaleur Bay,—
Sailed away from a sinking wreck,
With his own town's-people on her deck!
"Lay by! lay by!" they called to him.
Back he answered, "Sink or swim!
Brag of your catch of fish again!"
And off he sailed through the fog and rain!
    Old Floyd Ireson, for his hard heart,
    Tarred and feathered and carried in a cart
    By the women of Marblehead!

Fathoms deep in dark Chaleur
That wreck shall lie forevermore.
Mother and sister, wife and maid,
Looked from the rocks of Marblehead
Over the moaning and rainy sea,—
Looked for the coming that might not be!
What did the winds and the sea-birds say
Of the cruel captain who sailed away?—
   Old Floyd Ireson, for his hard heart,
   Tarred and feathered and carried in a cart
   By the women of Marblehead!

Through the street, on either side,
Up flew windows, doors swung wide;
Sharp-tongued spinsters, old wives gray,
Treble lent the fish-horn's bray.
Sea-worn grandsires, cripple-bound,
Hulks of old sailors run aground,
Shook head, and fist, and hat, and cane,
And cracked with curses the hoarse refrain:
   "Here's Flud Oirson, fur his horrd horrt,
   Torr'd an' futherr'd an' corr'd in a corrt
   By the women o' Morble'ead!"

Sweetly along the Salem road
Bloom of orchard and lilac showed.
Little the wicked skipper knew
Of the fields so green and the sky so blue.
Riding there in his sorry trim,
Like an Indian idol glum and grim,
Scarcely he seemed the sound to hear
Of voices shouting, far and near:
   "Here's Flud Oirson, fur his horrd horrt,

Torr'd en' futherr'd an' corr'd in a corrt
By the women o' Morble'ead!"

"Hear me, neighbors!" at last he cried,—
"What to me is this noisy ride?
What is the shame that clothes the skin
To the nameless horror that lives within?
Waking or sleeping, I see a wreck,
And hear a cry from a reeling deck!
Hate me and curse me,—I only dread
The hand of God and the face of the dead!"
    Said old Floyd Ireson, for his hard heart,
    Tarred and feathered and carried in a cart
        By the women of Marblehead!

Then the wife of the skipper lost at sea
Said, "God has touched him! why should we!"
Said an old wife mourning her only son,
"Cut the rogue's tether and let him run!"
So with soft relentings and rude excuse,
Half scorn, half pity, they cut him loose,
And gave him a cloak to hide him in,
And left him alone with his shame and sin.
    Poor Floyd Ireson, for his hard heart,
    Tarred and feathered and carried in a cart
        By the women of Marblehead!

1857

What should we do with a poem such as "Mabel Martin"?

Maybe just let ourselves enjoy it. True, it is not the kind of poem that a mainstream literary journal would publish today. It is too long and maybe even too predictable. In a way, it is little better than a nineteenth-century version of a made-for-television movie. But here is the catch: sometimes a romantic movie—with only the most tenuous tie to reality—is just what we want. Even in its melodrama, there is something nevertheless appealing in a story of love and goodness, where innocence finds protection and loneliness is lost in love. And as usual, Whittier's craft is sure: his vivid images of the cornhusking and courtship create verisimilitude enough for the realist in us.

Mabel Martin

A HARVEST IDYL

Susanna Martin, an aged woman of Amesbury, Mass., was tried and executed for the alleged crime of witchcraft. Her home was in what is now known as Pleasant Valley on the Merrimac, a little above the old Ferry way, where, tradition says, an attempt was made to assassinate Sir Edmund Andros on his way to Falmouth (afterward Portland) and Pemaquid, which was frustrated by a warning timely given. Goody Martin was the only woman hanged on the north side of the Merrimac during the dreadful delusion. The aged wife of Judge Bradbury, who lived on the other side of the Powow River, was imprisoned and would have been put to death but for the collapse of the hideous persecution.

The substance of the poem which follows was published under the name of *The Witch's Daughter*, in *The National Era* in 1857. In 1875 my publishers

desired to issue it with illustrations, and I then
enlarged it and otherwise altered it to its present
form. The principal addition was in the verses
which constitute Part I.

PROEM

I CALL the old time back: I bring my lay
In tender memory of the summer day
When, where our native river lapsed away,

We dreamed it over, while the thrushes made
Songs of their own, and the great pine-trees
   laid
On warm noonlights the masses of their shade.

And *she* was with us, living o'er again
Her life in ours, despite of years and pain,—
The Autumn's brightness after latter rain.

Beautiful in her holy peace as one
Who stands, at evening, when the work is
   done,
Glorified in the setting of the sun!

Her memory makes our common landscape
   seem
Fairer than any of which painters dream;
Lights the brown hills and sings in every stream;

For she whose speech was always truth's pure
   gold
Heard, not unpleased, its simple legends told,
And loved with us the beautiful and old.

I. THE RIVER VALLEY

Across the level tableland,
   A grassy, rarely trodden way,
   With thinnest skirt of birchen spray

And stunted growth of cedar, leads
   To where you see the dull plain fall
   Sheer off, steep-slanted, ploughed by all

The seasons' rainfalls. On its brink
   The over-leaning harebells swing,
   With roots half bare the pine-trees cling;

And, through the shadow looking west,
   You see the wavering river flow
   Along a vale, that far below

Holds to the sun, the sheltering hills
   And glimmering water-line between,
   Broad fields of corn and meadows green,

And fruit-bent orchards grouped around
   The low brown roofs and painted eaves,
   And chimney-tops half hid in leaves.

No warmer valley hides behind
   Yon wind-scourged sand-dunes, cold and
      bleak;
   No fairer river comes to seek

The wave-sung welcome of the sea,
   Or mark the northmost border line
   Of sun-loved growths of nut and vine.

183

Here, ground-fast in their native fields,
   Untempted by the city's gain,
   The quiet farmer folk remain

Who bear the pleasant name of Friends,
   And keep their fathers' gentle ways
   And simple speech of Bible days;

In whose neat homesteads woman holds
   With modest ease her equal place,
   And wears upon her tranquil face

The look of one who, merging not
   Her self-hood in another's will,
   Is love's and duty's handmaid still.

Pass with me down the path that winds
   Through birches to the open land,
   Where, close upon the river strand

You mark a cellar, vine o'errun,
   Above whose wall of loosened stones
   The sumach lifts its reddening cones,

And the black nightshade's berries shine,
   And broad, unsightly burdocks fold
   The household ruin, century-old.

Here, in the dim colonial time
   Of sterner lives and gloomier faith,
   A woman lived, tradition saith,

Who wrought her neighbors foul annoy,
　　And witched and plagued the countryside,
　　Till at the hangman's hand she died.

Sit with me while the westering day
　　Falls slantwise down the quiet vale,
　　And, haply ere yon loitering sail,

That rounds the upper headland, falls
　　Below Deer Island's pines, or sees
　　Behind it Hawkswood's belt of trees

Rise black against the sinking sun,
　　My idyl of its days of old,
　　The valley's legend, shall be told.

II. THE HUSKING

It was the pleasant harvest-time,
　　When cellar-bins are closely stowed,
　　And garrets bend beneath their load,

And the old swallow-haunted barns,—
　　Brown-gabled, long, and full of seams
　　Through which the moted sunlight streams,

And winds blow freshly in, to shake
　　The red plumes of the roosted cocks,
　　And the loose hay-mow's scented locks,—

Are filled with summer's ripened stores,
　　Its odorous grass and barley sheaves,
　　From their low scaffolds to their eaves.

On Esek Harden's oaken floor,
   With many an autumn threshing worn,
   Lay the heaped ears of unhusked corn.

And thither came young men and maids,
   Beneath a moon that, large and low,
   Lit that sweet eve of long ago.

They took their places; some by chance,
   And others by a merry voice
   Or sweet smile guided to their choice.

How pleasantly the rising moon,
   Between the shadow of the mows,
   Looked on them through the great elm-
      boughs!

On sturdy boyhood, sun-embrowned,
   On girlhood with its solid curves
   Of healthful strength and painless nerves!

And jests went round, and laughs that made
   The house-dog answer with his howl,
   And kept astir the barn-yard fowl;

And quaint old songs their fathers sung
   In Derby dales and Yorkshire moors,
   Ere Norman William trod their shores;

And tales, whose merry license shook
   The fat sides of the Saxon thane,
   Forgetful of the hovering Dane,—

Rude plays to Celt and Cimbri known,
    The charms and riddles that beguiled
    On Oxus' banks the young world's child,—

That primal picture-speech wherein
    Have youth and maid the story told,
    So new in each, so dateless old,

Recalling pastoral Ruth in her
    Who waited, blushing and demure,
    The red-ear's kiss of forfeiture.

III. THE WITCH'S DAUGHTER

But still the sweetest voice was mute
    That river-valley ever heard
    From lips of maid or throat of bird;

For Mabel Martin sat apart,
    And let the hay-mow's shadow fall
    Upon the loveliest face of all.

She sat apart, as one forbid,
    Who knew that none would condescend
    To own the Witch-wife's child a friend.

The seasons scarce had gone their round,
    Since curious thousands thronged to see
    Her mother at the gallows-tree;

And mocked the prison-palsied limbs
    That faltered on the fatal stairs,
    And wan lip trembling with its prayers!

Few questioned of the sorrowing child,
  Or, when they saw the mother die,
  Dreamed of the daughter's agony.

They went up to their homes that day,
  As men and Christians justified:
  God willed it, and the wretch had died!

Dear God and Father of us all,
  Forgive our faith in cruel lies,—
  Forgive the blindness that denies!

Forgive thy creature when he takes,
  For the all-perfect love Thou art,
  Some grim creation of his heart.

Cast down our idols, overturn
  Our bloody altars; let us see
  Thyself in Thy humanity!

Young Mabel from her mother's grave
  Crept to her desolate hearth-stone,
  And wrestled with her fate alone;

With love, and anger, and despair,
  The phantoms of disordered sense,
  The awful doubts of Providence!

Oh, dreary broke the winter days,
  And dreary fell the winter nights
  When, one by one, the neighboring lights

Went out, and human sounds grew still,
   And all the phantom-peopled dark
   Closed round her hearth-fire's dying spark.

And summer days were sad and long,
   And sad the uncompanioned eves,
   And sadder sunset-tinted leaves,

And Indian Summer's airs of balm;
   She scarcely felt the soft caress,
   The beauty died of loneliness!

The school-boys jeered her as they passed,
   And, when she sought the house of prayer,
   Her mother's curse pursued her there.

And still o'er many a neighboring door
   She saw the horseshoe's curvëd charm,
   To guard against her mother's harm:

That mother, poor and sick and lame,
   Who daily, by the old arm-chair,
   Folded her withered hands in prayer;—

Who turned, in Salem's dreary jail,
   Her worn old Bible o'er and o'er,
   When her dim eyes could read no more!

Sore tried and pained, the poor girl kept
   Her faith, and trusted that her way,
   So dark, would somewhere meet the day.

And still her weary wheel went round
    Day after day, with no relief:
    Small leisure have the poor for grief.

IV. THE CHAMPION

So in the shadow Mabel sits;
    Untouched by mirth she sees and hears,
    Her smile is sadder than her tears.

But cruel eyes have found her out,
    And cruel lips repeat her name,
    And taunt her with her mother's shame.

She answered not with railing words,
    But drew her apron o'er her face,
    And, sobbing, glided from the place.

And only pausing at the door,
    Her sad eyes met the troubled gaze
    Of one who, in her better days,

Had been her warm and steady friend,
    Ere yet her mother's doom had made
    Even Esek Harden half afraid.

He felt that mute appeal of tears,
    And, starting, with an angry frown,
    Hushed all the wicked murmurs down.

"Good neighbors mine," he sternly said,
    "This passes harmless mirth or jest;
    I brook no insult to my guest.

"She is indeed her mother's child,
But God's sweet pity ministers
Unto no whiter soul than hers.

"Let Goody Martin rest in peace;
I never knew her harm a fly,
And witch or not, God knows—not I.

"I know who swore her life away;
And as God lives, I'd not condemn
An Indian dog on word of them."

The broadest lands in all the town,
The skill to guide, the power to awe,
Were Harden's; and his word was law.

None dared withstand him to his face,
But one sly maiden spake aside:
"The little witch is evil-eyed!

"Her mother only killed a cow,
Or witched a churn or dairy-pan;
But she, forsooth, must charm a man!"

V. IN THE SHADOW

Poor Mabel, homeward turning, passed
The nameless terrors of the wood,
And saw, as if a ghost pursued,

Her shadow gliding in the moon;
The soft breath of the west-wind gave
A chill as from her mother's grave.

How dreary seemed the silent house!
  Wide in the moonbeams' ghastly glare
  Its windows had a dead man's stare!

And, like a gaunt and spectral hand,
  The tremulous shadow of a birch
  Reached out and touched the door's low
      porch,

As if to lift its latch; hard by,
  A sudden warning call she heard,
  The night-cry of a boding bird.

She leaned against the door; her face,
  So fair, so young, so full of pain,
  White in the moonlight's silver rain.

The river, on its pebbled rim,
  Made music such as childhood knew;
  The door-yard tree was whispered through

By voices such as childhood's ear
  Had heard in moonlights long ago;
  And through the willow-boughs below

She saw the rippled waters shine;
  Beyond, in waves of shade and light,
  The hills rolled off into the night.

She saw and heard, but over all
  A sense of some transforming spell,
  The shadow of her sick heart fell.

And still across the wooded space
    The harvest lights of Harden shone,
    And song and jest and laugh went on.

And he, so gentle, true, and strong,
    Of men the bravest and the best,
    Had he, too, scorned her with the rest?

She strove to drown her sense of wrong,
    And, in her old and simple way,
    To teach her bitter heart to pray.

Poor child! the prayer, begun in faith,
    Grew to a low, despairing cry
    Of utter misery: "Let me die!

"Oh! take me from the scornful eyes,
    And hide me where the cruel speech
    And mocking finger may not reach!

"I dare not breathe my mother's name:
    A daughter's right I dare not crave
    To weep above her unblest grave!

"Let me not live until my heart,
    With few to pity, and with none
    To love me, hardens into stone.

"O God! have mercy on Thy child,
    Whose faith in Thee grows weak and small,
    And take me ere I lose it all!"

A shadow on the moonlight fell,
  And murmuring wind and wave became
  A voice whose burden was her name.

VI. THE BETROTHAL

Had then God heard her? Had He sent
  His angel down? In flesh and blood,
  Before her Esek Harden stood!

He laid his hand upon her arm:
  "Dear Mabel, this no more shall be;
  Who scoffs at you must scoff at me.

"You know rough Esek Harden well;
  And if he seems no suitor gay,
  And if his hair is touched with gray,

"The maiden grown shall never find
  His heart less warm than when she smiled,
  Upon his knees a little child!"

Her tears of grief were tears of joy,
  As, folded in his strong embrace,
  She looked in Esek Harden's face.

"O truest friend of all!" she said,
  "God bless you for your kindly thought,
  And make me worthy of my lot!"

He led her forth, and, blent in one,
  Beside their happy pathway ran
  The shadows of the maid and man.

He led her through his dewy fields,
    To where the swinging lanterns glowed,
    And through the doors the huskers showed.

"Good friends and neighbors!" Esek said,
    "I'm weary of this lonely life;
    In Mabel see my chosen wife!

"She greets you kindly, one and all;
    The past is past, and all offence
    Falls harmless from her innocence.

"Henceforth she stands no more alone;
    You know what Esek Harden is;—
    He brooks no wrong to him or his.

"Now let the merriest tales be told,
    And let the sweetest songs be sung
    That ever made the old heart young!

"For now the lost has found a home;
    And a lone hearth shall brighter burn,
    As all the household joys return!"

Oh, pleasantly the harvest-moon,
    Between the shadow of the mows,
    Looked on them through the great elm-
        boughs!

On Mabel's curls of golden hair,
    On Esek's shaggy strength it fell;
    And the wind whispered, "It is well!"

                                        1857

As a student of religious history, Whittier knew well that the era of witch trials was a dark time indeed, far darker than the final effect of "The Witch of Wenham." The dramatic, too-easy escape and especially the unlikely, too-cute passing remark—"He does not know, she whispered low, / A little witch am I"—should not, however, make us overlook the poem's greater truth. In this narrative a mother who fears losing her son fabricates evidence for an accusation, evidence that the professional witch-hunter is only too glad to confirm with community rumor. Whittier thus demonstrates that the evil that plagues humans is often of our own making.

And just as important, the poet's craft is once again superb: he creates a literary ballad that manages to sound traditional through its vivid images, dramatic dialogue, and graphic action. If there is a flaw, it may be less the melodrama than the tendency, like many of Whittier's songs, to depart from the ballad tradition by making too strong a didactic appeal. Yet his appeal is one still worth hearing.

The Witch of Wenham

The house is still standing in Danvers, Mass., where, it is said, a suspected witch was confined overnight in the attic, which was bolted fast. In the morning, when the constable came to take her to Salem for trial, she was missing, although the door

was still bolted. Her escape was doubtless aided by
her friends, but at the time it was attributed to
Satanic interference.

I

ALONG Crane River's sunny slopes
 Blew warm the winds of May,
And over Naumkeag's ancient oaks
 The green outgrew the gray.

The grass was green on Rial-side,
 The early birds at will
Waked up the violet in its dell,
 The wind-flower on its hill.

"Where go you, in your Sunday coat,
 Son Andrew, tell me, pray."
"For stripëd perch in Wenham Lake
 I go to fish to-day."

"Unharmed of thee in Wenham Lake
 The mottled perch shall be:
A blue-eyed witch sits on the bank
 And weaves her net for thee.

"She weaves her golden hair; she sings
 Her spell-song low and faint;
The wickedest witch in Salem jail
 Is to that girl a saint."

"Nay, mother, hold thy cruel tongue;
 God knows," the young man cried,
"He never made a whiter soul
 Than hers by Wenham side.

"She tends her mother sick and blind,
    And every want supplies;
To her above the blessed Book
    She lends her soft blue eyes.

"Her voice is glad with holy songs,
    Her lips are sweet with prayer;
Go where you will, in ten miles round
    Is none more good and fair."

"Son Andrew, for the love of God
    And of thy mother, stay!"
She clasped her hands, she wept aloud,
    But Andrew rode away.

"O reverend sir, my Andrew's soul
    The Wenham witch has caught;
She holds him with the curlëd gold
    Whereof her snare is wrought.

"She charms him with her great blue eyes,
    She binds him with her hair;
Oh, break the spell with holy words,
    Unbind him with a prayer!"

"Take heart," the painful preacher said,
    "This mischief shall not be;
The witch shall perish in her sins
    And Andrew shall go free.

"Our poor Ann Putnam testifies
    She saw her weave a spell,
Bare-armed, loose-haired, at full of moon,
    Around a dried-up well.

" 'Spring up, O well!' she softly sang
   The Hebrew's old refrain
(For Satan uses Bible words),
   Till water flowed amain.

"And many a goodwife heard her speak
   By Wenham water words
That made the buttercups take wings
   And turn to yellow birds.

"They say that swarming wild bees seek
   The hive at her command;
And fishes swim to take their food
   From out her dainty hand.

"Meek as she sits in meeting-time,
   The godly minister
Notes well the spell that doth compel
   The young men's eyes to her.

"The mole upon her dimpled chin
   Is Satan's seal and sign;
Her lips are red with evil bread
   And stain of unblest wine.

"For Tituba, my Indian, saith
   At Quasycung she took
The Black Man's godless sacrament
   And signed his dreadful book.

"Last night my sore-afflicted child
   Against the young witch cried.
To take her Marshal Herrick rides
   Even now to Wenham side."

The marshal in his saddle sat,
   His daughter at his knee;
"I go to fetch that arrant witch,
   Thy fair playmate," quoth he.

"Her spectre walks the parsonage,
   And haunts both hall and stair;
They know her by the great blue eyes
   And floating gold of hair."

"They lie, they lie, my father dear!
   No foul old witch is she,
But sweet and good and crystal-pure
   As Wenham waters be."

"I tell thee, child, the Lord hath set
   Before us good and ill,
And woe to all whose carnal loves
   Oppose His righteous will.

"Between Him and the powers of hell
   Choose thou, my child, to-day:
No sparing hand, no pitying eye,
   When God commands to slay!"

He went his way; the old wives shook
   With fear as he drew nigh;
The children in the dooryards held
   Their breath as he passed by.

Too well they knew the gaunt gray horse
   The grim witch-hunter rode,
The pale Apocalyptic beast
   By grisly Death bestrode.

II

Oh, fair the face of Wenham Lake
  Upon the young girl's shone,
Her tender mouth, her dreaming eyes
  Her yellow hair outblown.

By happy youth and love attuned
  To natural harmonies,
The singing birds, the whispering wind,
  She sat beneath the trees.

Sat shaping for her bridal dress
  Her mother's wedding gown,
When lo! the marshal, writ in hand,
  From Alford hill rode down.

His face was hard with cruel fear,
  He grasped the maiden's hands:
"Come with me unto Salem town,
  For so the law commands!"

"Oh, let me to my mother say
  Farewell before I go!"
He closer tied her little hands
  Unto his saddle bow.

"Unhand me," cried she piteously,
  "For thy sweet daughter's sake."
"I'll keep my daughter safe," he said,
  "From the witch of Wenham Lake."

"Oh, leave me for my mother's sake,
  She needs my eyes to see."

"Those eyes, young witch, the crows shall peck
    From off the gallows-tree."

He bore her to a farm-house old
    And up its stairway long,
And closed on her the garret-door
    With iron bolted strong.

The day died out, the night came down:
    Her evening prayer she said,
While, through the dark, strange faces seemed
    To mock her as she prayed.

The present horror deepened all
    The fears her childhood knew;
The awe wherewith the air was filled
    With every breath she drew.

And could it be, she trembling asked,
    Some secret thought or sin
Had shut good angels from her heart
    And let the bad ones in?

Had she in some forgotten dream
    Let go her hold on Heaven,
And sold herself unwittingly
    To spirits unforgiven?

Oh, weird and still the dark hours passed;
    No human sound she heard,
But up and down the chimney stack
    The swallows moaned and stirred.

And o'er her, with a dread surmise
 Of evil sight and sound,
The blind bats on their leathern wings
 Went wheeling round and round.

Low hanging in the midnight sky
 Looked in a half-faced moon.
Was it a dream, or did she hear
 Her lover's whistled tune?

She forced the oaken scuttle back;
 A whisper reached her ear:
"Slide down the roof to me," it said,
 "So softly none may hear."

She slid along the sloping roof
 Till from its eaves she hung,
And felt the loosened shingles yield
 To which her fingers clung.

Below, her lover stretched his hands
 And touched her feet so small;
"Drop down to me, dear heart," he said,
 "My arms shall break the fall."

He set her on his pillion soft,
 Her arms about him twined;
And, noiseless as if velvet-shod,
 They left the house behind.

But when they reached the open way,
 Full free the rein he cast;
Oh, never through the mirk midnight
 Rode man and maid more fast.

Along the wild wood-paths they sped,
  The bridgeless streams they swam;
At set of moon they passed the Bass,
  At sunrise Agawam.

At high noon on the Merrimac
  The ancient ferryman
Forgot, at times, his idle oars,
  So fair a freight to scan.

And when from off his grounded boat
  He saw them mount and ride,
"God keep her from the evil eye,
  And harm of witch!" he cried.

The maiden laughed, as youth will laugh
  At all its fears gone by;
"He does not know," she whispered low,
  "A little witch am I."

All day he urged his weary horse,
  And, in the red sundown,
Drew rein before a friendly door
  In distant Berwick town.

A fellow-feeling for the wronged
  The Quaker people felt;
And safe beside their kindly hearths
  The hunted maiden dwelt,

Until from off its breast the land
  The haunting horror threw,
And hatred, born of ghastly dreams,
  To shame and pity grew.

Sad were the year's spring morns, and sad
   Its golden summer day,
But blithe and glad its withered fields,
   And skies of ashen gray;

For spell and charm had power no more,
   The spectres ceased to roam,
And scattered households knelt again
   Around the hearths of home.

And when once more by Beaver Dam
   The meadow-lark outsang,
And once again on all the hills
   The early violets sprang,

And all the windy pasture slopes
   Lay green within the arms
Of creeks that bore the salted sea
   To pleasant inland farms,

The smith filed off the chains he forged,
   The jail-bolts backward fell;
And youth and hoary age came forth
   Like souls escaped from hell.

1877

Though he often spun poetry from legend, Whittier sometimes grounded his work on stories he loved for their historical truth. And his knowledge of Quaker history was a ready supply of

fact as strange as fiction. The early days of the
Friends movement in America offered many
instances in which believers were moved to outra-
geous methods of speaking the truth, and certainly
the story of Margaret Brewster is one of the more
compelling. "With a look the old-time sibyls wore,
/ Half-crazed and half-divine," she responds to the
Holy Spirit's promptings by dressing in sackcloth
and ashes and railing against the evils of clerical-
ism. And where better to do so than squarely in
the middle of a "steeple-house"?

In the "Old South"

On the 8th of July, 1677, Margaret Brewster
with four other Friends went into the South
Church in time of meeting, "in sackcloth, with
ashes upon her head, barefoot, and her face
blackened," and delivered "a warning from the
great God of Heaven and Earth to the Rulers and
Magistrates of Boston." For the offence she was
sentenced to be "whipped at a cart's tail up and
down the Town, with twenty lashes."

SHE came and stood in the Old South Church,
    A wonder and a sign,
With a look the old-time sibyls wore,
    Half-crazed and half-divine.

Save the mournful sackcloth about her
        wound,
    Unclothed as the primal mother,
With limbs that trembled and eyes that blazed
    With a fire she dare not smother.

Loose on her shoulders fell her hair,
　　With sprinkled ashes gray;
She stood in the broad aisle strange and weird
　　As a soul at the judgment day.

And the minister paused in his sermon's
　　　　midst,
　　And the people held their breath,
For these were the words the maiden spoke
　　Through lips as the lips of death:

"Thus saith the Lord, with equal feet
　　All men my courts shall tread,
And priest and ruler no more shall eat
　　My people up like bread!

"Repent! repent! ere the Lord shall speak
　　In thunder and breaking seals!
Let all souls worship Him in the way
　　His light within reveals."

She shook the dust from her naked feet,
　　And her sackcloth closer drew,
And into the porch of the awe-hushed church
　　She passed like a ghost from view.

They whipped her away at the tail o' the cart
　　Through half the streets of the town,
But the words she uttered that day nor fire
　　Could burn nor water drown.

And now the aisles of the ancient church
　　By equal feet are trod,
And the bell that swings in its belfry rings
　　Freedom to worship God!

207

And now whenever a wrong is done
    It thrills the conscious walls;
The stone from the basement cries aloud
    And the beam from the timber calls.

There are steeple-houses on every hand,
    And pulpits that bless and ban,
And the Lord will not grudge the single church
    That is set apart for man.

For in two commandments are all the law
    And the prophets under the sun,
And the first is last and the last is first,
    And the twain are verily one.

So long as Boston shall Boston be,
    And her bay-tides rise and fall,
Shall freedom stand in the Old South Church
    And plead for the rights of all!

                         1877

Many people mistakenly suppose that religious freedom in America began at Plymouth Rock. But that is far from true, and in no colonial scene was religion less free than in Whittier's native Massachusetts. Like "In the 'Old South,'" "The King's Missive" is an historical tale that voices the poet's passion for Quaker history and his admiration for Friends who were faithful in the face of Puritan persecution. As Whittier admits, his details have been disputed, but he tried to be true to the historical facts as he knew them. And the affirmation that sounds the poem's final note—"the freedom of soul he prophesied / Is gospel and law where the martyrs died"— is characteristic of Whittier's faith in the final victory of goodness.

The King's Missive
1661

This ballad, originally written for *The Memorial History of Boston*, describes, with pardonable poetic license, a memorable incident in the annals of the city. The interview between Shattuck and the Governor took place, I have since learned, in the residence of the latter, and not in the Council Chamber. The publication of the ballad led to some discussion as to the historical truthfulness of the picture, but I have seen no reason to rub out any of the figures or alter the lines and colors.

UNDER the great hill sloping bare
    To cove and meadow and Common lot,
In his council chamber and oaken chair,
    Sat the worshipful Governor Endicott.
A grave, strong man, who knew no peer
In the pilgrim land, where he ruled in fear
Of God, not man, and for good or ill
Held his trust with an iron will.

He had shorn with his sword the cross from out
    The flag, and cloven the May-pole down,
Harried the heathen round about,
    And whipped the Quakers from town to town.

209

Earnest and honest, a man at need
To burn like a torch for his own harsh creed,
He kept with the flaming brand of his zeal
The gate of the holy common weal.

His brow was clouded, his eye was stern,
    With a look of mingled sorrow and wrath;
"Woe's me!" he murmured: "at every turn
    The pestilent Quakers are in my path!
Some we have scourged, and banished some,
Some hanged, more doomed, and still they
                come,
Fast as the tide of yon bay sets in,
Sowing their heresy's seed of sin.

"Did we count on this? Did we leave behind
    The graves of our kin, the comfort and ease
Of our English hearths and homes, to find
    Troublers of Israel such as these?
Shall I spare? Shall I pity them? God forbid!
I will do as the prophet to Agag did:
They come to poison the wells of the Word,
I will hew them in pieces before the Lord!"

The door swung open, and Rawson the clerk
    Entered, and whispered under breath,
"There waits below for the hangman's work
    A fellow banished on pain of death—
Shattuck, of Salem, unhealed of the whip,
Brought over in Master Goldsmith's ship
At anchor here in a Christian port,
With freight of the devil and all his sort!"

Twice and thrice on the chamber floor
   Striding fiercely from wall to wall,
"The Lord do so to me and more,"
   The Governor cried, "if I hang not all!
Bring hither the Quaker." Calm, sedate,
With the look of a man at ease with fate,
Into that presence grim and dread
Came Samuel Shattuck, with hat on head.

"Off with the knave's hat!" An angry hand
   Smote down the offence; but the wearer said,
With a quiet smile, "By the king's command
   I bear his message and stand in his stead."
In the Governor's hand a missive he laid
With the royal arms on its seal displayed,
And the proud man spake as he gazed thereat,
Uncovering, "Give Mr. Shattuck his hat."

He turned to the Quaker, bowing low,—
   "The king commandeth your friends' release;
Doubt not he shall be obeyed, although
   To his subjects' sorrow and sin's increase.
What he here enjoineth, John Endicott,
His loyal servant, questioneth not.
You are free! God grant the spirit you own
May take you from us to parts unknown."

So the door of the jail was open cast,
   And, like Daniel, out of the lion's den
Tender youth and girlhood passed,
     With age-bowed women and gray-locked
       men.
And the voice of one appointed to die

Was lifted in praise and thanks on high,
And the little maid from New Netherlands
Kissed, in her joy, the doomed man's hands.

And one, whose call was to minister
   To the souls in prison, beside him went,
An ancient woman, bearing with her
   The linen shroud for his burial meant.
For she, not counting her own life dear,
In the strength of a love that cast out fear,
Had watched and served where her brethren
       died,
Like those who waited the cross beside.

One moment they paused on their way to look
   On the martyr graves by the Common side,
And much scourged Wharton of Salem took
   His burden of prophecy up and cried:
"Rest, souls of the valiant! Not in vain
Have ye borne the Master's cross of pain;
Ye have fought the fight, ye are victors
       crowned,
With a fourfold chain ye have Satan bound!"

The autumn haze lay soft and still
   On wood and meadow and upland farms;
On the brow of Snow Hill the great windmill
   Slowly and lazily swung its arms;
Broad in the sunshine stretched away,
With its capes and islands, the turquoise bay;
And over water and dusk of pines
Blue hills lifted their faint outlines.

The topaz leaves of the walnut glowed,
   The sumach added its crimson fleck,
And double in air and water showed
   The tinted maples along the Neck;
Through frost flower clusters of pale star-mist,
And gentian fringes of amethyst,
And royal plumes of golden-rod,
The grazing cattle on Centry trod.

But as they who see not, the Quakers saw
   The world about them; they only thought
With deep thanksgiving and pious awe
   On the great deliverance God had wrought.
Through lane and alley the gazing town
Noisily followed them up and down;
Some with scoffing and brutal jeer,
Some with pity and words of cheer.

One brave voice rose above the din.
   Upsall, gray with his length of days,
Cried from the door of his Red Lion Inn:
   "Men of Boston, give God the praise!
No more shall innocent blood call down
The bolts of wrath on your guilty town.
The freedom of worship, dear to you,
Is dear to all, and to all is due.

"I see the vision of days to come,
   When your beautiful City of the Bay
Shall be Christian liberty's chosen home,
   And none shall his neighbor's rights gainsay.
The varying notes of worship shall blend
And as one great prayer to God ascend,
And hands of mutual charity raise
Walls of salvation and gates of praise."

213

So passed the Quakers through Boston town,
    Whose painful ministers sighed to see
The walls of their sheep-fold falling down,
    And wolves of heresy prowling free.
But the years went on, and brought no wrong;
With milder counsels the State grew strong,
As outward Letter and inward Light
Kept the balance of truth aright.

The Puritan spirit perishing not,
    To Concord's yeomen the signal sent,
And spake in the voice of the cannon-shot
    That severed the chains of a continent.
With its gentler mission of peace and goodwill
The thought of the Quaker is living still,
And the freedom of soul he prophesied
Is gospel and law where the martyrs died.

1881

Whittier's optimistic view of humankind burns through clearly, even in this ballad which tells a cruel and perverse story. Once again the heroes of the poem are faithful Quaker witnesses: three women being whipped from town to town by order of Richard Waldron. Yet the focus of Whittier's narrative is not on Waldron's depravity, but on the clear thinking and heroism of a handful of folks along the way—first a child, then a poor old woman, and, finally, Justice Pike of Salisbury.

It was important to Whittier to tell these old tales of Christian faithfulness, but it was just as important not to respond hatefully, even to

Puritans long dead. The key to the poet's perspective is revealed in these lines, as he relates that

> The tale is one of an evil time,
> When souls were fettered and thought was crime,
> And heresy's whisper above its breath
> Meant shameful scourging and bonds and death.

Characteristically, Whittier portrayed this cruel era as a time long gone. Though we may consider him too optimistic, his refusal to vilify or condemn those who had persecuted his spiritual forbears reveals the very center of his faith.

How the Women Went from Dover

The following is a copy of the warrant issued by Major Waldron, of Dover, in 1662. The Quakers, as was their wont, prophesied against him, and saw, as they supposed, the fulfilment of their prophecy when, many years after, he was killed by the Indians.

To the constables of Dover, Hampton, Salisbury, Newbury, Rowley, Ipswich, Wenham, Lynn, Boston, Roxbury, Dedham, and until these vagabond Quakers are carried out of this jurisdiction.

You, and every one of you, are required, in the King's Majesty's name, to take these vagabond Quakers, Anne Colman, Mary Tompkins, and Alice Ambrose, and make them fast to the cart's tail, and driving the cart through your several towns, to whip them upon their naked backs not exceeding ten stripes apiece on each of them, in each town; and so to convey them from constable to constable

till they are out of this jurisdiction, as you will
answer it at your peril, and this shall be your
warrant.

RICHARD WALDRON.

Dated at Dover, December 22, 1662.

This warrant was executed only in Dover and
Hampton. At Salisbury the constable refused to
obey it. He was sustained by the town's people,
who were under the influence of Major Robert
Pike, the leading man in the lower valley of the
Merrimac, who stood far in advance of his time, as
an advocate of religious freedom and an opponent
of ecclesiastical authority. He had the moral courage
to address an able and manly letter to the court at
Salem, remonstrating against the witchcraft trials.

THE tossing spray of Cocheco's fall
Hardened to ice on its rocky wall,
As through Dover town in the chill, gray dawn,
Three women passed, at the cart-tail drawn!

Bared to the waist, for the north wind's grip
And keener sting of the constable's whip,
The blood that followed each hissing blow
Froze as it sprinkled the winter snow.

Priest and ruler, boy and maid
Followed the dismal cavalcade;
And from door and window, open thrown
Looked and wondered gaffer and crone.

"God is our witness," the victims cried,
"We suffer for Him who for all men died;
The wrong ye do has been done before,
We bear the stripes that the Master bore!

"And thou, O Richard Waldron, for whom
We hear the feet of a coming doom,
On thy cruel heart and thy hand of wrong
Vengeance is sure, though it tarry long.

"In the light of the Lord, a flame we see
Climb and kindle a proud roof-tree;
And beneath it an old man lying dead,
With stains of blood on his hoary head."

"Smite, Goodman Hate - Evil!—harder still!"
The magistrate cried, "lay on with a will!
Drive out of their bodies the Father of Lies,
Who through them preaches and prophesies!"

So into the forest they held their way,
By winding river and frost-rimmed bay,
Over wind-swept hills that felt the beat
Of the winter sea at their icy feet.

The Indian hunter, searching his traps,
Peered stealthily through the forest gaps;
And the outlying settler shook his head,—
"They're witches going to jail," he said.

At last a meeting-house came in view;
A blast on his horn the constable blew;
And the boys of Hampton cried up and down
"The Quakers have come!" to the wondering
            town.

From barn and woodpile the goodman came;
The goodwife quitted her quilting frame,

With her child at her breast; and, hobbling
  slow,
The grandam followed to see the show.

Once more the torturing whip was swung,
Once more keen lashes the bare flesh stung.
"Oh, spare! they are bleeding!" a little maid
  cried,
And covered her face the sight to hide.

A murmur ran round the crowd: "Good folks,"
Quoth the constable, busy counting the strokes,
"No pity to wretches like these is due,
They have beaten the gospel black and blue!"

Then a pallid woman, in wild-eyed fear,
With her wooden noggin of milk drew near.
"Drink, poor hearts!" a rude hand smote
Her draught away from a parching throat.

"Take heed," one whispered, "they'll take
  your cow
For fines, as they took your horse and plough,
And the bed from under you." "Even so,"
She said; "they are cruel as death, I know."

Then on they passed, in the waning day,
Through Seabrook woods, a weariful way;
By great salt meadows and sand-hills bare,
And glimpses of blue sea here and there.

By the meeting-house in Salisbury town,
The sufferers stood, in the red sundown,

Bare for the lash! O pitying Night,
Drop swift thy curtain and hide the sight!

With shame in his eye and wrath on his lip
The Salisbury constable dropped his whip.
"This warrant means murder foul and red;
Cursed is he who serves it," he said.

"Show me the order, and meanwhile strike
A blow at your peril!" said Justice Pike.
Of all the rulers the land possessed,
Wisest and boldest was he and best.

He scoffed at witchcraft; the priest he met
As man meets man; his feet he set
Beyond his dark age, standing upright,
Soul-free, with his face to the morning light.

He read the warrant: *"These convey*
From our precincts; at every town on the way
Give each ten lashes." "God judge the brute!
I tread his order under my foot!

"Cut loose these poor ones and let them go;
Come what will of it, all men shall know
No warrant is good, though backed by the
                    Crown
For whipping women in Salisbury town!"

The hearts of the villagers, half released
From creed of terror and rule of priest,
By a primal instinct owned the right
Of human pity in law's despite.

For ruth and chivalry only slept,
His Saxon manhood the yeoman kept;
Quicker or slower, the same blood ran
In the Cavalier and the Puritan.

The Quakers sank on their knees in praise
And thanks. A last, low sunset blaze
Flashed out from under a cloud, and shed
A golden glory on each bowed head.

The tale is one of an evil time,
When souls were fettered and thought was
        crime,
And heresy's whisper above its breath
Meant shameful scourging and bonds and
        death!

What marvel, that hunted and sorely tried,
Even woman rebuked and prophesied,
And soft words rarely answered back
The grim persuasion of whip and rack!

If her cry from the whipping-post and jail
Pierced sharp as the Kenite's driven nail,
O woman, at ease in these happier days,
Forbear to judge of thy sister's ways!

How much thy beautiful life may owe
To her faith and courage thou canst not know,
Nor how from the paths of thy calm retreat
She smoothed the thorns with her bleeding feet.

                          1883

Another tale of religious persecution, in this narrative Quakers are once again driven from their home by those whose "zeal for God / Was cruelty to man." Though he writes about the Puritans with kindness, the irony of the situation was not lost on Whittier: he compares the exiles from Massachusetts to the very pilgrims who had settled in the Bay State not fifty years before, having come in search of freedom to live out their religious faith. He notes, and quite logically, that in persecuting the Friends, the Puritans "did / Anew the wrong their Pilgrim Fathers bore!" Neither is the poet blind to the effect that such a sordid history has on the present, as he ends, "Oh mother State, how foiled was thy design! / The gain was theirs, the loss alone was thine." His emphasis, however, is not on the historical evil but on the heritage of faithfulness.

Banished From Massachusetts 1660

On a painting by E. A. Abbey. The General Court of Massachusetts enacted Oct. 19, 1658, that "any person or persons of the cursed sect of Quakers" should, on conviction of the same, be banished, on pain of death, from the jurisdiction of the commonwealth.

Over the threshold of his pleasant home
    Set in green clearings passed the exiled Friend,

In simple trust, misdoubting not the end.
"Dear heart of mine!" he said, "the time has come
To trust the Lord for shelter." One long gaze
   The goodwife turned on each familiar thing,—
   The lowing kine, the orchard blossoming,
The open door that showed the hearth-fire's
          blaze,—
And calmly answered, "Yes, He will provide."
   Silent and slow they crossed the homestead's
          bound,
   Lingering the longest by their child's grave-
          mound.
   "Move on, or stay and hang!" the sheriff cried.
They left behind them more than home or land,
And set sad faces to an alien strand.

Safer with winds and waves than human wrath,
   With ravening wolves than those whose zeal for
          God
   Was cruelty to man, the exiles trod
Drear leagues of forest without guide or path,
Or launching frail boats on the uncharted sea,
   Round storm-vexed capes, whose teeth of
          granite ground
   The waves to foam, their perilous way they
          wound,
Enduring all things so their souls were free.
Oh, true confessors; shaming them who did
   Anew the wrong their Pilgrim Fathers bore!
   For you the Mayflower spread her sail once more,
Freighted with souls, to all that duty bid
Faithful as they who sought an unknown land,
O'er wintry seas, from Holland's Hook of Sand!

So from his lost home to the darkening main,
    Bodeful of storm, stout Macy held his way,
    And, when the green shore blended with the
            gray,
His poor wife moaned: "Let us turn back again."
"Nay, woman, weak of faith, kneel down," said he,
    "And say thy prayers: the Lord himself will steer;
    And led by Him, nor man nor devils I fear!"
So the gray Southwicks, from a rainy sea,
Saw, far and faint, the loom of land, and gave
    With feeble voices thanks for friendly ground
    Whereon to rest their weary feet, and found
A peaceful death-bed and a quiet grave
Where, ocean-walled, and wiser than his age,
The lord of Shelter scorned the bigot's rage.

Aquidneck's isle, Nantucket's lonely shores,
    And Indian-haunted Narragansett saw
    The way-worn travellers round their camp-fire
            draw,
Or heard the plashing of their weary oars.
And every place whereon they rested grew
    Happier for pure and gracious womanhood,
    And men whose names for stainless honor
            stood,
Founders of States and rulers wise and true.
The Muse of history yet shall make amends
    To those who freedom, peace, and justice taught,
    Beyond their dark age led the van of thought,
And left unforfeited the name of Friends.
O mother State, how foiled was thy design!
The gain was theirs, the loss alone was thine.

1884

223

V.
Tokens of an
Inward Journey

"Trust" and Other Lessons

To put the matter kindly, much contemporary poetry is frank, personal, and confessional. To put the same matter darkly, much contemporary poetry is self-absorbed, and obsessively so. For good, for ill, or for both, Whittier's body of work stands in sharp relief against such a backdrop: through much of his career, he was a public poet with a public message.

But sometimes, by intention or the reflective nature of his craft, he led readers on a revealing saunter within his soul. Thankfully, he did so often enough to suggest a compelling collage, a study in fragments of a deeply spiritual life. Some of the poems in this section will, without a doubt, hold their place among the best devotional poetry ever written. They bear lasting witness to the subtle passion of Whittier's craft, to his concern for his fellow humans, and to the gracious depth of his insight.

Love, in one way or another, is the theme of Whittier's most thoroughly religious poetry—hardly surprising for a man whose last words were these: "Love—love to all the world." Though the shape love takes varies considerably, the best of this work concentrates on God's relationship with—and God revealing Godself to—humans. A traditional Quaker throughout his life, the poet's expression of this relationship is naturally revealed in the language of Friends. The worship he celebrates is the worship of the "gathered meeting," the theology he regards most highly is that in which all argument resolves in the love of God, and the revelation he regards most highly is not in a Bible or ecstatic vision but in "The Word," the spirit which speaks to the individual. If early in his career Whittier was ill at ease with the subject areas of his fellow romantics, and if in his political poems his focus necessarily took an outward and secular turn, here those tensions are at rest. In the best of the religious poems, we experience the mature artist focusing directly on those religious issues most important to his life. The result is what may be the finest religious poetry of his place and time—the crowning achievement of a life that meaningfully integrated personal conviction, social responsibility, and the art of poetry, practiced at a high level.

The simple poem "Forgiveness" provides important insight into the calm, constant, even reasonable nature of Whittier's faith. The speaker in the poem, having been wronged, forgives, but not because of some outpouring of deeply felt love for the offender. Neither is he motivated by a spiritual, mystical prompting. The poem conveys strong emotion as a good lyric must, but its emo-

tion is initiated by the poet's own intense iden-
tification with the plight of his race—with what it
means to be human, and, therefore, fallible. It is
that "common sorrow," he tells us, that "swept all
my pride away," making forgiveness possible.

Forgiveness

My heart was heavy, for its trust had been
    Abused, its kindness answered with foul wrong;
So, turning gloomily from my fellow-men,
    One summer Sabbath day I strolled among
The green mounds of the village burial-place;
    Where, pondering how all human love and hate
    Find one sad level; and how, soon or late,
Wronged and wrongdoer, each with meekened face,
    And cold hands folded over a still heart,
Pass the green threshold of our common grave,
    Whither all footsteps tend, whence none depart,
Awed for myself, and pitying my race,
Our common sorrow, like a mighty wave,
Swept all my pride away, and trembling I forgave!

1847

Whittier was not only a Quaker, he was very
Quaker, so very Quaker that long after many
of his contemporaries had dropped the peculiarities
of the sect, he held not only to the beliefs but even
to the speech and dress of the Friends. It is to his

credit, then, that he seldom seems narrow or
sectarian in his writing. His liberality is due in part
to the principles of Quakerism—one of its tenets
remains an openness to all God's truth, whatever
its source. But just as importantly, those aspects of
Whittier's belief that he chooses to celebrate most
openly are in fact attractive to most devoutly
religious people. One needn't be a Quaker or even
a Christian to value, in the quiet of worship, the
old familiar places and the faces of fellow believers.
And one needn't be a Quaker to celebrate "the still
small voice"— or to read upon one's heart "a still
diviner law."

First-Day Thoughts

In calm and cool and silence, once again
   I find my old accustomed place among
   My brethren, where, perchance, no human
                tongue
   Shall utter words; where never hymn is sung,
   Nor deep-toned organ blown, nor censer swung,
Nor dim light falling through the pictured pane!
There, syllabled by silence, let me hear
The still small voice which reached the prophet's ear;
Read in my heart a still diviner law
Than Israel's leader on his tables saw!
There let me strive with each besetting sin,
   Recall my wandering fancies, and restrain
   The sore disquiet of a restless brain;
   And, as the path of duty is made plain,
May grace be given that I may walk therein,
   Not like the hireling, for his selfish gain,

With backward glances and reluctant tread,
Making a merit of his coward dread,
   But, cheerful, in the light around me thrown,
   Walking as one to pleasant service led;
   Doing God's will as if it were my own,
Yet trusting not in mine, but in His strength alone!

1853

Whittier's work is rich with references to scriptures. In fact, his knowledge of the Bible—and his use of it—may be greater than that of any other American poet. But in this poem, written to celebrate a gift from a friend, Whittier goes beyond the biblical stories for some happy conjecture, thus doing a little myth-making of his own. In Whittier's version of the banishment from the garden, a stern angel pities Eve and gives her a slip of a tree. Apparently the angel "[f]orgave the lovely trespasser and turned / Aside his face of fire." But Whittier's playfulness has limits: even in his fancy, that bit of "primal good," the perfection demonstrated in his friend's gift, reminds readers of what was lost with Adam's fall.

The Fruit-Gift

LAST night, just as the tints of autumn's sky
   Of sunset faded from our hills and streams,
   I sat, vague listening, lapped in twilight dreams,
To the leaf's rustle, and the cricket's cry.

Then, like that basket, flush with summer fruit,
Dropped by the angels at the Prophet's foot,
Came, unannounced, a gift of clustered sweetness,
   Full-orbed, and glowing with the prisoned beams
Of summery suns, and rounded to completeness
By kisses of the south-wind and the dew.
Thrilled with a glad surprise, methought I knew
The pleasure of the homeward-turning Jew,
When Eshcol's clusters on his shoulders lay,
Dropping their sweetness on his desert way.

I said, "This fruit beseems no world of sin.
   Its parent vine, rooted in Paradise,
   O'ercrept the wall, and never paid the price
   Of the great mischief,—an ambrosial tree,
Eden's exotic, somehow smuggled in,
   To keep the thorns and thistles company."
Perchance our frail, sad mother plucked in haste
   A single vine-slip as she passed the gate,
Where the dread sword alternate paled and burned,
   And the stern angel, pitying her fate,
Forgave the lovely trespasser, and turned
Aside his face of fire; and thus the waste
And fallen world hath yet its annual taste
Of primal good, to prove of sin the cost,
And show by one gleaned ear the mighty harvest
      lost.

              1856

In Whittier's day, the pool of easy Christian belief, at least for intellectuals, was quickly evaporating.

And many folks who did maintain a living faith sought religious expression far outside the pale of traditional orthodoxy. Yet Whittier maintained to the end beliefs about as orthodox as a Quaker's beliefs could be—he put his faith in a knowing and knowable God who loved His creation. Gracefully, the poet managed to steer clear of religious dogma while maintaining a faith that nurtured not only his own spirit, but, in turn, allowed him to nurture the many pilgrims drawn by his fame. This humble constancy in the face of the unknown makes him as attractive a counselor to us today as he was to his contemporaries.

Trust

THE same old baffling questions! O my friend,
I cannot answer them. In vain I send
My soul into the dark, where never burn
    The lamps of science, nor the natural light
Of Reason's sun and stars! I cannot learn
Their great and solemn meanings, nor discern
The awful secrets of the eyes which turn
    Evermore on us through the day and night
    With silent challenge and a dumb demand,
Proffering the riddles of the dread unknown,
Like the calm Sphinxes, with their eyes of stone,
    Questioning the centuries from their veils of sand!
I have no answer for myself or thee,
Save that I learned beside my mother's knee;
"All is of God that is, and is to be;
    And God is good." Let this suffice us still,

Resting in childlike trust upon His will
Who moves to His great ends unthwarted by the ill.

1853

L ike many of his less orthodox contemporaries,
Whittier believed in the improvement of
religion—that is, he believed that religious truth
would be understood better and acted upon more
fully as civilizations developed. Indeed, some
elements of Christianity that would to many, even
today, remain sacrosanct, were to Whittier the
vestiges of an older, less developed faith. This
position must be kept in mind as one reads
Whittier's frequent comments on the ancient
creeds, those ideas that "[t]he poor creed-mongers
dreamed and guessed." Given such a stance, it is
little wonder that such a doctrine as the Trinity
would eventually gain his attention.
Characteristically, Whittier fills the old concept
with a new understanding that does not deny
"orthodoxy," but which does turn an abstraction
into a useful lesson for faithful living.

Trinitas

AT morn I prayed, "I fain would see
How Three are One, and One is Three;
Read the dark riddle unto me."

I wandered forth, the sun and air
I saw bestowed with equal care
On good and evil, foul and fair.

No partial favor dropped the rain;
Alike the righteous and profane
Rejoiced above their heading grain.

And my heart murmured, "Is it meet
That blindfold Nature thus should treat
With equal hand the tares and wheat?"

A presence melted through my mood,—
A warmth, a light, a sense of good,
Like sunshine through a winter wood.

I saw that presence, mailed complete
In her white innocence, pause to greet
A fallen sister of the street.

Upon her bosom snowy pure
The lost one clung, as if secure
From inward guilt or outward lure.

"Beware!" I said; "in thus I see
No gain to her, but loss to thee:
Who touches pitch defiled must be."

I passed the haunts of shame and sin,
And a voice whispered, "Who therein
Shall these lost souls to Heaven's peace win?

"Who there shall hope and health dispense,
And lift the ladder up from thence
Whose rounds are prayers of penitence?"

I said, "No higher life they know;
These earth-worms love to have it so.
Who stoops to raise them sinks as low."

That night with painful care I read
What Hippo's saint and Calvin said;
The living seeking to the dead!

In vain I turned, in weary quest,
Old pages, where (God give them rest!)
The poor creed-mongers dreamed and
                  guessed.

And still I prayed, "Lord, let me see
How Three are One, and One is Three;
Read the dark riddle unto me!"

Then something whispered, "Dost thou pray
For what thou hast? This very day
The Holy Three have crossed thy way.

"Did not the gifts of sun and air
To good and ill alike declare
The all-compassionate Father's care?

"In the white soul that stooped to raise
The lost one from her evil ways,
Thou saw'st the Christ, whom angels praise!

"A bodiless Divinity,
The still small Voice that spake to thee
Was the Holy Spirit's mystery!

"O blind of sight, of faith how small!
Father, and Son, and Holy Call;
This day thou hast denied them all!

"Revealed in love and sacrifice,
The Holiest passed before thine eyes,
One and the same, in threefold guise.

"The equal Father in rain and sun,
His Christ in the good to evil done,
His Voice in thy soul;—and the Three are One!"

I shut my grave Aquinas fast;
The monkish gloss of ages past,
The schoolman's creed aside I cast.

And my heart answered, "Lord, I see
How Three are One, and One is Three;
Thy riddle hath been read to me!"

1858

Whittier's mature faith is nowhere better reflected than in "My Psalm," as all the angles of his life are "slow rounding into calm." Though the poet was only 51 when this poem was published, it carries the tone of acceptance and reflection that testifies to a life well lived, its battles faithfully fought. It was written at a time when his most active political involvement had ceased, and he was approaching the fullness of his literary power. Having passed through youthful regret and finally looking—if from afar—toward death, the poet is at ease with his life and is thankful. Even the very end seems "but a covered way / which opens into light." It is worth noting, too, that this poem was written long before his financial success and before his broadest literary acclaim.

My Psalm

I MOURN no more my vanished years:
    Beneath a tender rain,
An April rain of smiles and tears,
    My heart is young again.

The west-winds blow, and, singing low,
    I hear the glad streams run;
The windows of my soul I throw
    Wide open to the sun.

No longer forward nor behind
    I look in hope or fear;
But, grateful, take the good I find,
    The best of now and here.

I plough no more a desert land,
    To harvest weed and tare;
The manna dropping from God's hand
    Rebukes my painful care.

I break my pilgrim staff, I lay
   Aside the toiling oar;
The angel sought so far away
   I welcome at my door.

The airs of spring may never play
   Among the ripening corn,
Nor freshness of the flowers of May
   Blow through the autumn morn;

Yet shall the blue-eyed gentian look
   Through fringëd lids to heaven,
And the pale aster in the brook
   Shall see its image given;—

The woods shall wear their robes of praise,
   The south-wind softly sigh,
And sweet, calm days in golden haze
   Melt down the amber sky.

Not less shall manly deed and word
   Rebuke an age of wrong;
The graven flowers that wreathe the sword
   Make not the blade less strong.

But smiting hands shall learn to heal,—
   To build as to destroy;
Nor less my heart for others feel
   That I the more enjoy.

All as God wills, who wisely heeds
   To give or to withhold,

And knoweth more of all my needs
   Than all my prayers have told!

Enough that blessings undeserved
   Have marked my erring track;
That wheresoe'er my feet have swerved,
   His chastening turned me back;

That more and more a Providence
   Of love is understood,
Making the springs of time and sense
   Sweet with eternal good;—

That death seems but a covered way
   Which opens into light,
Wherein no blinded child can stray
   Beyond the Father's sight;

That care and trial seem at last,
   Through Memory's sunset air,
Like mountain-ranges overpast,
   In purple distance fair;

That all the jarring notes of life
   Seem blending in a psalm,
And all the angles of its strife
   Slow rounding into calm.

And so the shadows fall apart,
   And so the west-winds play;
And all the windows of my heart
   I open to the day.

                1859

like his fellow American romantics, Whittier sought the divine in every prospect of nature. He valued the forests, hills, and pastures not only for their intrinsic beauty, but for what they revealed about his own soul. As a devout Friend, it is only natural that Whittier would frame epiphanies in nature as Christian truths. So when "sudden our pathway turned from night; / the hills swung open to the light," Whittier did not simply sense a mystical elevation. He experienced instead an affirmation of Christian doctrine: when occasionally freed from our doubts, our "eyes that fail on earth" can look forth on "eternal hills" where we see the "dear ones whom we loved below."

The River Path

No bird-song floated down the hill,
The tangled bank below was still;

No rustle from the birchen stem,
No ripple from the water's hem.

The dusk of twilight round us grew,
We felt the falling of the dew;

For, from us, ere the day was done,
The wooded hills shut out the sun.

241

But on the river's farther side
We saw the hill-tops glorified,—

A tender glow, exceeding fair,
A dream of day without its glare.

With us the damp, the chill, the gloom:
With them the sunset's rosy bloom;

While dark, through willowy vistas seen,
The river rolled in shade between.

From out the darkness where we trod,
We gazed upon those hills of God,

Whose light seemed not of moon or sun.
We spake not, but our thought was one.

We paused, as if from that bright shore
Beckoned our dear ones gone before;

And stilled our beating hearts to hear
The voices lost to mortal ear!

Sudden our pathway turned from night;
The hills swung open to the light;

Through their green gates the sunshine
        showed,
A long, slant splendor downward flowed.

Down glade and glen and bank it rolled;
It bridged the shaded stream with gold;

And, borne on piers of mist, allied
The shadowy with the sunlit side!

"So," prayed we, "when our feet draw near
The river dark, with mortal fear,

"And the night cometh chill with dew,
O Father! let Thy light break through!

"So let the hills of doubt divide,
So bridge with faith the sunless tide!

"So let the eyes that fail on earth
On Thy eternal hills look forth;

"And in Thy beckoning angels know
The dear ones whom we loved below!"

1860

At the center of Whittier's faith was a relationship with a God who knows and loves and who can be known and loved—experientially. "The Eternal Goodness" reveals Whittier at his most devotional, as he contrasts his own living faith with those who take a more mechanistic approach to the divine. And he is not simply defending his position: one can sense something like indignation in such lines as "Who fathoms the Eternal Thought? / Who talks of scheme and plan?" The God Whittier knows "needeth not / The poor

device of man." But, as was his custom, the poet
invested little ink in theological argument. The
goodness of God was the ground of Whittier's
theology, and his theology extended little beyond
that point. As a result there follows a simple
beauty in this affirmation which features some of
his most comforting quatrains, including the
timeless testimony, "I know not where His islands
lift / Their fronded palms in air; / I only know I
cannot drift / Beyond His love and care."

The Eternal Goodness

O FRIENDS! with whom my feet have trod
    The quiet aisles of prayer,
Glad witness to your zeal for God
    And love of man I bear.

I trace your lines of argument;
    Your logic linked and strong
I weigh as one who dreads dissent,
    And fears a doubt as wrong.

But still my human hands are weak
    To hold your iron creeds:
Against the words ye bid me speak
    My heart within me pleads.

Who fathoms the Eternal Thought?
    Who talks of scheme and plan?
The Lord is God! He needeth not
    The poor device of man.

I walk with bare, hushed feet the ground
  Ye tread with boldness shod;
I dare not fix with mete and bound
  The love and power of God.

Ye praise His justice; even such
  His pitying love I deem:
Ye seek a king; I fain would touch
  The robe that hath no seam.

Ye see the curse which overbroods
  A world of pain and loss;
I hear our Lord's beatitudes
  And prayer upon the cross.

More than your schoolmen teach, within
  Myself, alas! I know:
Too dark ye cannot paint the sin,
  Too small the merit show.

I bow my forehead to the dust,
  I veil mine eyes for shame,
And urge, in trembling self-distrust,
  A prayer without a claim.

I see the wrong that round me lies,
  I feel the guilt within;
I hear, with groan and travail-cries,
  The world confess its sin.

Yet, in the maddening maze of things,
  And tossed by storm and flood,
To one fixed trust my spirit clings;
  I know that God is good!

Not mine to look where cherubim
    And seraphs may not see,
But nothing can be good in Him
    Which evil is in me.

The wrong that pains my soul below
    I dare not throne above,
I know not of His hate,—I know
    His goodness and His love.

I dimly guess from blessings known
    Of greater out of sight,
And, with the chastened Psalmist, own
    His judgments too are right.

I long for household voices gone,
    For vanished smiles I long,
But God hath led my dear ones on,
    And He can do no wrong.

I know not what the future hath
    Of marvel or surprise,
Assured alone that life and death
    His mercy underlies.

And if my heart and flesh are weak
    To bear an untried pain,
The bruisëd reed He will not break,
    But strengthen and sustain.

No offering of my own I have,
    Nor works my faith to prove;
I can but give the gifts He gave,
    And plead His love for love.

And so beside the Silent Sea
   I wait the muffled oar;
No harm from Him can come to me
   On ocean or on shore.

I know not where His islands lift
   Their fronded palms in air;
I only know I cannot drift
   Beyond His love and care.

O brothers! if my faith is vain,
   If hopes like these betray,
Pray for me that my feet may gain
   The sure and safer way.

And Thou, O Lord! by whom are seen
   Thy creatures as they be,
Forgive me if too close I lean
   My human heart on Thee!

1865

In "The Clear Vision," Whittier seems strikingly modern in his understanding of personal perception. Since the poem begins with "I did but dream," we suspect that the "clear vision" may be something mystical or even miraculous. Instead, we discover quite the opposite, as the poet reflects, "*Within my heart* the change is wrought" (my emphasis). In other words, he realizes that it is his right but all too rare perception that reveals the world around him as "enchanted." Such a realization naturally turns the poet to prayer, and by the poem's end he addresses the Creator, "As thou hast made thy world without, / make thou more fair my world within."

The Clear Vision

I DID but dream. I never knew
    What charms our sternest season wore.
Was never yet the sky so blue,
    Was never earth so white before.
Till now I never saw the glow
Of sunset on yon hills of snow,
And never learned the bough's designs
Of beauty in its leafless lines.

Did ever such a morning break
    As that my eastern windows see?
Did ever such a moonlight take
    Weird photographs of shrub and tree?
Rang ever bells so wild and fleet
The music of the winter street?
Was ever yet a sound by half
So merry as yon school-boy's laugh?

O Earth! with gladness overfraught,
    No added charm thy face hath found;
Within my heart the change is wrought,
    My footsteps make enchanted ground.
From couch of pain and curtained room
Forth to thy light and air I come,
To find in all that meets my eyes
The freshness of a glad surprise.

Fair seem these winter days, and soon
　　Shall blow the warm west-winds of spring,
To set the unbound rills in tune
　　And hither urge the bluebird's wing.
The vales shall laugh in flowers, the woods
Grow misty green with leafing buds,
And violets and wind-flowers sway
Against the throbbing heart of May.

Break forth, my lips, in praise, and own
　　The wiser love severely kind;
Since, richer for its chastening grown,
　　I see, whereas I once was blind.
The world, O Father! hath not wronged
With loss the life by Thee prolonged;
But still, with every added year,
More beautiful Thy works appear!

As Thou hast made thy world without,
　　Make Thou more fair my world within;
Shine through its lingering clouds of doubt;
　　Rebuke its haunting shapes of sin;
Fill, brief or long, my granted span
Of life with love to thee and man;
Strike when thou wilt the hour of rest,
But let my last days be my best!

　　　　　　　　　　　　　　　1868

The feeling of having been guided by intuition, the sense that what ought to be strange is, instead, strangely familiar, is experienced by many

249

religious people. Whittier's "A Mystery" focuses on
that phenomenon, but without trying to over-
interpret the experience. On the contrary, he takes
comfort in the encounter, but he lets the mystery
stand: his response is not to explicate but to share
the peace he feels with change, the peace he feels
with his life on earth, the peace he feels in a
foreshadowing of heaven.

In this way, "A Mystery" contrasts nicely with
"The Pressed Gentian." In the second poem, the
"Christmas token," the gift he has received, does
become something of a text to be explicated. As
the poet interprets it, the ornament is a lesson for
those who see it from both sides; viewed from
within and without, it acts as a symbol for people
and things whose true, inner worth is veiled. Both
poems are well-crafted and moving in their
respective ways, and together they suggest the
complementary distinction between an affirming
mystical experience and a more reasoned spiritual
insight.

A Mystery

THE river hemmed with leaning trees
   Wound through its meadows green;
A low, blue line of mountains showed
   The open pines between.

One sharp, tall peak above them all
   Clear into sunlight sprang:
I saw the river of my dreams,
   The mountains that I sang!

No clue of memory led me on,
    But well the ways I knew;
A feeling of familiar things
    With every footstep grew.

Not otherwise above its crag
    Could lean the blasted pine;
Not otherwise the maple hold
    Aloft its red ensign.

So up the long and shorn foot-hills
    The mountain road should creep;
So, green and low, the meadow fold
    Its red-haired kine asleep.

The river wound as it should wind;
    Their place the mountains took;
The white torn fringes of their clouds
    Wore no unwonted look.

Yet ne'er before that river's rim
    Was pressed by feet of mine,
Never before mine eyes had crossed
    That broken mountain line.

A presence, strange at once and known,
    Walked with me as my guide;
The skirts of some forgotten life
    Trailed noiseless at my side.

Was it a dim-remembered dream?
    Or glimpse through aeons old?
The secret which the mountains kept
    The river never told.

But from the vision ere it passed
   A tender hope I drew,
And, pleasant as a dawn of spring,
   The thought within me grew,

That love would temper every change,
   And soften all surprise,
And, misty with the dreams of earth,
   The hills of Heaven arise.

1875

The Pressed Gentian

THE time of gifts has come again,
And, on my northern window-pane,
Outlined against the day's brief light,
A Christmas token hangs in sight.
The wayside travellers, as they pass,
Mark the gray disk of clouded glass;
And the dull blankness seems, perchance,
Folly to their wise ignorance.

They cannot from their outlook see
The perfect grace it hath for me;
For there the flower, whose fringes through
The frosty breath of autumn blew,
Turns from without its face of bloom
To the warm tropic of my room,
As fair as when beside its brook
The hue of bending skies it took.

So from the trodden ways of earth,
Seem some sweet souls who veil their worth,
And offer to the careless glance
The clouding gray of circumstance.
They blossom best where hearth-fires burn,
To loving eyes alone they turn
The flowers of inward grace, that hide
Their beauty from the world outside.

But deeper meanings come to me,
My half-immortal flower, from thee!
Man judges from a partial view,
None ever yet his brother knew;
The Eternal Eye that sees the whole
May better read the darkened soul,
And find, to outward sense denied,
The flower upon its inmost side!

1876

If you mention "The Word" to many Christians, they assume that you mean the Bible. But this is not uniformly the case. In Quaker tradition, "The Word" refers not to the Bible but to the guiding presence of Christ within, or as the old Friends often phrased it, the Inward Light; or, in Whittier's terms, the "Voice of the Holy Spirit, making known / Man to himself, a witness swift and sure." This distinction is continued still more clearly in "The Book." The Bible, Whittier believed, could be rightly read "only when on form and word obscure / Falls from above the white supernal light."

Together, these two poems demonstrate Whittier's Quaker understanding of scripture: one reads "The Book" with the guidance of "The Word."

The Word

VOICE of the Holy Spirit, making known
   Man to himself, a witness swift and sure,
   Warning, approving, true and wise and pure,
Counsel and guidance that misleadeth none!
By thee the mystery of life is read;
   The picture-writing of the world's gray seers,
   The myths and parables of the primal years,
Whose letter kills, by thee interpreted
Take healthful meanings fitted to our needs,
   And in the soul's vernacular express
   The common law of simple righteousness.
Hatred of cant and doubt of human creeds
May well be felt: the unpardonable sin
Is to deny the Word of God within!

1879

The Book

GALLERY of sacred pictures manifold
   A minster rich in holy effigies,
   And bearing on entablature and frieze
The hieroglyphic oracles of old.
Along its transept aureoled martyrs sit;

And the low chancel side-lights half acquaint
The eye with shrines of prophet, bard, and saint,
Their age-dimmed tablets traced in doubtful writ!
But only when on form and word obscure
　　Falls from above the white supernal light
　　We read the mystic characters aright,
And life informs the silent portraiture,
Until we pause at last, awe-held, before
The One ineffable Face, love, wonder, and adore.

　　　　　　　　　　　　　　1879

Whittier often found spiritual truths in nature, and we become so accustomed to anticipating the lesson that we can easily overlook something just as important: Whittier was a skilled observer of the natural world, and some of his descriptive writing is really excellent. In fact, the lesson of "The Trailing Arbutus" does not disappoint us; we can each recall some friend who, though in hard circumstances, nevertheless lent "sweetness to the ungenial day." But the exacting description of the arbutus and its place in the woods reminds us that this farmer's son spent a good portion of his youth striding through the meadows and woods, and was so attuned to nature's subtleties that he could be led to a particular flower, "guided by its sweet / Perfume."

The Trailing Arbutus

I WANDERED lonely where the pine-trees made
Against the bitter East their barricade,
   And, guided by its sweet
Perfume, I found, within a narrow dell,
The trailing spring flower tinted like a shell
   Amid dry leaves and mosses at my feet.

From under dead boughs, for whose loss the pines
Moaned ceaseless overhead, the blossoming vines
   Lifted their glad surprise,
While yet the bluebird smoothed in leafless trees
His feathers ruffled by the chill sea-breeze,
   And snow-drifts lingered under April skies.

As, pausing, o'er the lonely flower I bent,
I thought of lives thus lowly, clogged and pent,
   Which yet find room,
Through care and cumber, coldness and decay,
To lend a sweetness to the ungenial day,
   And make the sad earth happier for their bloom.

1880

If this non-creedal Quaker could be accused of
having a creed, here it is.

"Requirement" is the heart of Whittier's
theology. The poet uses traditional Christian
language—"We live by Faith"—but quickly adds
that "Faith is not the slave / Of text and legend." In

other words, Whittier suggests that one's own practice of true religion need not be validated by a particular understanding of an ancient text. The essence of true faith, the faith that leads to a "life that stands as all true lives have stood, / Firm-rooted in the faith that God is good," is what the Divine requires, not a precise interpretation of dogma or adherence to a unique theological system. Throughout his life the poet's conviction stood firm: whatever is essential to true religion is illumined by the Spirit within.

Requirement

WE live by Faith; but Faith is not the slave
    Of text and legend. Reason's voice and God's,
    Nature's and Duty's, never are at odds.
What asks our Father of His children, save
Justice and mercy and humility,
    A reasonable service of good deeds,
    Pure living, tenderness to human needs,
Reverence and trust, and prayer for light to see
The Master's footprints in our daily ways?
    No knotted scourge nor sacrificial knife,
    But the calm beauty of an ordered life
Whose very breathing is unworded praise!—
A life that stands as all true lives have stood,
Firm-rooted in the faith that God is Good.

                        1881

As a "people's poet," Whittier gave voice to what many of his neighbors and countrymen were thinking and feeling. His contemporaries were deeply interested in life beyond the grave, and his era experienced a swelling of interest not only in millennial understandings of Christianity, but in seances, mediums, and all kinds of paranormal research. Almost everyone, it seemed, sought some kind of proof, emotional or empirical, that death was not the end. In "At Last," Whittier addresses this concern with a poem that is a prayer, a simple request that God be present in death as God has been in life. The final stanza, however, hints at something more. It reveals Whittier's sense that we long for something that can never be attained in our life, that we have tasted a hint of something better that can never be fully realized here. That realization can only come in the life to be found "beneath [God's] trees of healing."

At Last

WHEN on my day of life the night is falling,
    And, in the winds from unsunned spaces
        blown,
I hear far voices out of darkness calling
    My feet to paths unknown,

Thou who hast made my home of life so
    pleasant,
  Leave not its tenant when its walls decay;
O Love Divine, O Helper ever present,
  Be Thou my strength and stay!

Be near me when all else is from me drifting;
  Earth, sky, home's pictures, days of shade
    and shine,
And kindly faces to my own uplifting
  The love which answers mine.

I have but Thee, my Father! let Thy spirit
  Be with me then to comfort and uphold;
No gate of pearl, no branch of palm I merit,
  Nor street of shining gold.

Suffice it if—my good and ill unreckoned,
  And both forgiven through Thy abounding
    grace—
I find myself by hands familiar beckoned
  Unto my fitting place.

Some humble door among Thy many
    mansions,
  Some sheltering shade where sin and
    striving cease,
And flows forever through heaven's green
    expansions
  The river of Thy peace.

There, from the music round about me
    stealing,
I fain would learn the new and holy song,
And find at last, beneath Thy trees of healing,
    The life for which I long.

1882

Nineteenth-century Americans faced many challenging changes: innovations in science, new industrial technologies, and shifting economics were rapidly rewriting the pages of their lives. For some this meant the dissolution of faith; for others it brought about a retreat into religious fundamentalism. To his credit, Whittier avoided both fruitless extremes. Though he felt keenly some of the confusion and anxiety of his countrymen, he was sustained by an unwavering faith in the "Inward Word." "Truth," he tells us in this poem, "has charmed life." Though theological understanding may change, those things that really matter, "faith, hope, and charity," are not so easily shaken. Humans must adjust their understandings, to be sure, but the Truth is constant. I like to think that maybe today Whittier has joined, in his own words, those "clear-eyed saints [who] look down / Untroubled on the wreck of schemes and creeds."

Adjustment

THE tree of Faith its bare, dry boughs must shed
   That nearer heaven the living ones may climb;
   The false must fail, though from our shores of
          time
The old lament be heard, "Great Pan is dead!"
That wail is Error's, from his high place hurled;
   This sharp recoil is Evil undertrod;
   Our time's unrest, an angel sent of God
Troubling with life the waters of the world.
Even as they list the winds of the Spirit blow
   To turn or break our century-rusted vanes;
   Sands shift and waste; the rock alone remains
Where, led of Heaven, the strong tides come and go,
And storm-clouds, rent by thunderbolt and wind,
Leave, free of mist, the permanent stars behind.

Therefore I trust, although to outward sense
   Both true and false seem shaken; I will hold
   With newer light my reverence for the old
And calmly wait the births of Providence.
No gain is lost; the clear-eyed saints look down
   Untroubled on the wreck of schemes and creeds;
   Love yet remains, its rosary of good deeds
Counting in task-field and o'erpeopled town.
Truth has charmed life; the Inward Word survives,
   And, day by day, its revelation brings;
   Faith, hope, and charity, whatsoever things
Which cannot be shaken, stand. Still holy lives
Reveal the Christ of whom the letter told,
And the new gospel verifies the old.

1884

True religion for Whittier centered on those principles which are eternal; his faith set little store by the particulars of place and time. Such a stance, common enough in mystical religion, informs "The Christmas of 1888." In this poem, Whittier details a religious desire that defies all limitations, stepping lightly over centuries and continents with equal ease. Suddenly, through the practice of the poet's craft, Christmas seems closer: the same sun that shone on the Christ child rises and falls on us, the hills of Massachusetts grow as beautiful as those of Palestine, and the hunger of the faithful remains forever constant. Thus the Christian "heart's desire" parallels the "angels' midnight psalm": "Peace, and good-will to men!"

The Christmas of 1888

Low in the east, against a white, cold dawn,
The black-lined silhouette of the woods was drawn,
   And on a wintry waste
Of frosted streams and hillsides bare and brown,
Through thin cloud-films a pallid ghost looked down,
   The waning moon half-faced!

In that pale sky and sere, snow-waiting earth,
What sign was there of the immortal birth?
   What herald of the One?
Lo! swift as thought the heavenly radiance came,

A rose-red splendor swept the sky like flame,
   Up rolled the round, bright sun!

And all was changed. From a transfigured world
The moon's ghost fled, the smoke of home-hearths
          curled
   Up the still air unblown.
In Orient warmth and brightness, did that morn
O'er Nain and Nazareth, when the Christ was born,
   Break fairer than our own?

The morning's promise noon and eve fulfilled
In warm, soft sky and landscape hazy-hilled
   And sunset fair as they;
A sweet reminder of His holiest time,
A summer-miracle in our winter clime,
   God gave a perfect day.

The near was blended with the old and far,
And Bethlehem's hillside and the Magi's star
   Seemed here, as there and then,—
Our homestead pine-tree was the Syrian palm,
Our heart's desire the angels' midnight psalm,
   Peace, and good-will to men!

                     1888

Like the whiteness of Melville's great whale and the placid surface of Thoreau's Walden Pond, the glow of a drift-wood fire becomes for Whittier the focus of his most centered contemplation. Gazing into the flames, he suffers the passing of youthful desires—for fame, for political power, for the love of a woman. He seems glad, even, to dismiss such longings, and resigns himself to "turn from all that only seems, /And seek the sober grounds of truth." What once had seemed losses are now providentially revealed to have been "gains," and we sense that the poet is enjoying the coda of a life well lived. Yet Whittier is too much the traditional Christian to see death simply as the end. He knows "whence the airs have blown. /That whisper of the Eternal Sea," and he is ready to go there, to settle at last among the "Isles of Peace."

Burning Drift-Wood

BEFORE my drift-wood fire I sit,
    And see, with every waif I burn,
Old dreams and fancies coloring it,
    And folly's unlaid ghosts return.

O ships of mine, whose swift keels cleft
    The enchanted sea on which they sailed,
Are these poor fragments only left
    Of vain desires and hopes that failed?

Did I not watch from them the light
    Of sunset on my towers in Spain,
And see, far off, uploom in sight
    The Fortunate Isles I might not gain?

Did sudden lift of fog reveal
   Arcadia's vales of song and spring,
And did I pass, with grazing keel,
   The rocks whereon the sirens sing?

Have I not drifted hard upon
   The unmapped regions lost to man,
The cloud-pitched tents of Prester John,
   The palace domes of Kubla Khan?

Did land winds blow from jasmine flowers,
   Where Youth the ageless Fountain fills?
Did Love make sign from rose blown bowers,
   And gold from Eldorado's hills?

Alas! the gallant ships, that sailed
   On blind Adventure's errand sent,
Howe'er they laid their courses, failed
   To reach the haven of Content.

And of my ventures, those alone
   Which Love had freighted, safely sped,
Seeking a good beyond my own,
   By clear-eyed Duty piloted.

O mariners, hoping still to meet
   The luck Arabian voyagers met,
And find in Bagdad's moonlit street,
   Haroun al Raschid walking yet,

Take with you, on your Sea of Dreams,
   The fair, fond fancies dear to youth.

I turn from all that only seems,
    And seek the sober grounds of truth.

What matter that it is not May,
    That birds have flown, and trees are bare,
That darker grows the shortening day,
    And colder blows the wintry air!

The wrecks of passion and desire,
    The castles I no more rebuild,
May fitly feed my drift-wood fire,
    And warm the hands that age has chilled.

Whatever perished with my ships,
    I only know the best remains;
A song of praise is on my lips
    For losses which are now my gains.

Heap high my hearth! No worth is lost:
    No wisdom with the folly dies.
Burn on, poor shreds, your holocaust
    Shall be my evening sacrifice!

Far more than all I dared to dream,
    Unsought before my door I see;
On wings of fire and steeds of steam
    The world's great wonders come to me,

And holier signs, unmarked before,
    Of Love to seek and Power to save,—
The righting of the wronged and poor,
    The man evolving from the slave;

And life, no longer chance or fate,
   Safe in the gracious Fatherhood.
I fold o'er-wearied hands and wait,
   In full assurance of the good.

And well the waiting time must be,
   Though brief or long its granted days,
If Faith and Hope and Charity
   Sit by my evening hearth-fire's blaze.

And with them, friends whom Heaven has
      spared,
   Whose love my heart has comforted,
And, sharing all my joys, has shared
   My tender memories of the dead,—

Dear souls who left us lonely here,
   Bound on their last, long voyage, to whom
We, day by day, are drawing near,
   Where every bark has sailing room.

I know the solemn monotone
   Of waters calling unto me;
I know from whence the airs have blown
   That whisper of the Eternal Sea.

As low my fires of drift-wood burn,
   I hear that sea's deep sounds increase,
And, fair in sunset light, discern
   Its mirage-lifted Isles of Peace.

                  1890

Selected Bibliography

Selected Bibliography

Works by Whittier
The Writings of John Greenleaf Whittier. 7 vols. Boston:
     Houghton Mifflin, 1888-9. (Riverside Edition)
The Complete Poetical Works of John Greenleaf Whittier. Ed.
     Horace E. Scudder. Boston and New York: Houghton
     Mifflin, 1894. (Cambridge Edition)
The Letters of John Greenleaf Whittier. 3 vols. Ed. John B.
     Pickard. Cambridge: Harvard-Belknap, 1975.

Bibliography, Biography, and Criticism
Boswell, Jeanetta. *The Schoolroom Poets: A Bibliography of
     Bryant, Holmes, Longfellow, Lowell, and Whittier with
     Selective Annotation.* Metuchen, NJ: Scarecrow, 1983.
Clark, Harry Hayden. "The Growth of Whittier's Mind—
     Three Phases." *Emerson Society Quarterly* 50 (1968):
     119-26.
Currier, Thomas Franklin. *A Bibliography of John
     Greenleaf Whittier.* Cambridge: Harvard UP, 1937.
Jones, Rufus M. *The Faith of John Greenleaf Whittier.* New
     England Yearly Meeting of Friends, 1957.
Kribbs, Jayne K. *Critical Essays on John Greenleaf Whittier.*
     Boston: G. K. Hall, 1980.
Leary, Lewis. *John Greenleaf Whittier.* Twayne United
     States Authors Series. General Editor Sylvia E.
     Bowman. New York: Twayne, 1961.
Meek, Frederic M. "Whittier The Religious Man."
     Emerson Society Quarterly 50 (1968): 86-92.

Pickard, John B. *John Greenleaf Whittier: An Introduction and Interpretation*. New York: Holt, Rinehart and Winston, 1961.

--- .*Memorabilia of John Greenleaf Whittier*. Hartford: The Emerson Society, 1968.

---., ed. *Whittier Newsletter.* Haverill, MA, since 1966.

Pickard, Samuel T. *Life and Letters of John Greenleaf Whittier.* 2 vols. Boston: Houghton Mifflin, 1894.

---.*Whittier-Land, A Handbook of North Essex.* Boston: Houghton Mifflin, 1904.

Mordell, Albert. *Quaker Militant: John Greenleaf Whittier.* Boston: Houghton Mifflin, 1933.

Pollard, John. *John Greenleaf Whittier: Friend of Man.* Boston: Houghton Mifflin, 1949.

Rocks, James E. "Whittier's *Snow-Bound*: "The Circle Of Our Hearth" and the Discourse on Domesticity." *Studies in the American Renaissance* (1993): 339-353.

Smythe, Daniel W. "Whittier and the New Critics." *Emerson Society Quarterly* 50 (1968): 22-6.

Wagenknecht, Edward. *John Greenleaf Whittier: A Portrait In Paradox.* New York: Oxford, 1967.

Waggoner, Hyatt H. Introduction. *The Poetical Works of Whittier.* By John Greenleaf Whittier. Boston: Houghton Mifflin, 1975. Cambridge Edition.

Warren, Robert Penn. *John Greenleaf Whittier's Poetry: An Appraisal and a Selection.* Minneapolis: U of Minnesota P, 1971.

Woodall, Roland H. *John Greenleaf Whittier: A Biography.* Haverhill, MA: Trustees of the John Greenleaf Whittier Homestead, 1985.

Printed in the United States
70961LV00002B/319-399

9 780944 350485